D1596349

FEUDALISM

FEUDALISM

JOSEPH R. STRAYER

Dayton-Stockton Professor of History
Princeton University

AN ANVIL ORIGINAL

under the general editorship of

LOUIS L. SNYDER

VAN NOSTRAND REINHOLD COMPANY

NEW YORK CINCINNATI TORONTO
LONDON MELBOURNE

To the Memory
of
E. HARRIS HARBISON

VAN NOSTRAND REINHOLD COMPANY REGIONAL OFFICES:
Cincinnati New York Chicago Millbrae Dallas

VAN NOSTRAND REINHOLD COMPANY
INTERNATIONAL OFFICES:
London Toronto Melbourne

Published by VAN NOSTRAND REINHOLD COMPANY
450 West 33rd Street, New York, N.Y. 10001

Published simultaneously in Canada by
D. VAN NOSTRAND COMPANY (CANADA), LTD.

12 11 10 9 8 7 6 5 4

PREFACE

This book could be written only because great scholars for over three centuries have devoted themselves to the study of feudalism. Our own generation of historians has been especially fertile in new insights and new interpretations, and I owe much to the men whose works are listed in the recommended readings. My debt is especially great to Professor F. L. Ganshof, the dean of all living students of feudalism.

My own interpretation stresses feudalism as a method of government, and emphasizes the distinction between the great lords who had extensive political power, and the lesser vassals who were at first merely soldiers. In order to make these points clear I have translated a number of documents not commonly cited in studies of feudalism. For the same reason I have made my own translations from the original sources even when I was using familiar documents, since the translator's choice of words inevitably reflects his ideas about the nature of feudalism. I have probably not avoided bias, but I hope that I have achieved consistency, since in only one case (*Reading No. 35*) have I used the version of another scholar.

The dedication recalls long evenings of conversation with an old friend and colleague, whose wise and penetrating mind helped sharpen many of my ideas about the historical process. It is a small acknowledgement of a great obligation.

JOSEPH R. STRAYER

TABLE OF CONTENTS

Part I

FEUDALISM

— 1 —

INTRODUCTION

Feudalism is a difficult word. It was invented in the seventeenth century, at a time when the social phenomena it purported to describe had either vanished or were decaying rapidly. The men of the Middle Ages, who were deeply involved in what we call feudalism, never used the word, so that we cannot work out a definition from their statements. Modern scholars have long argued about the meaning of the term, without ever reaching agreement. Laymen have used it loosely, often as a way of condemning any political, economic, or social relationships they did not like. No definition will satisfy everyone, and yet we must have a tentative definition in order to know what we are talking about and what kind of behavior we are trying to describe.

Origin of the Term. We might start by remembering why the word was invented. The seventeenth-century lawyers and antiquarians who first used the term were either perplexed or fascinated by the survival of certain customs and institutions which were difficult to harmonize with prevailing legal and political theories. Restraints on royal power, the possession of public authority by private persons, peculiar rules about the use and transfer of real property, did not seem to fit with the concept of the sovereign state, the doctrine of divine right, or ideas about the sanctity of private property. It was also clear that these survivals did not go back to the classical period; they were just as repugnant to the spirit of Roman law as they were to the absolutism of the seventeenth century. They must, then, have originated in the Middle Ages, and most of them seemed to be connected with the medieval institution of the fief. Hence they were lumped together under the name of feudalism.[1] And the antiquarians who tried to explain the term, or the lawyers who tried to justify the peculiar rights of their clients, knew perfectly well where to find the explanations or justifications they needed: they began to examine with greater and greater care the legal and administrative records of medieval governments.

The first descriptions of feudalism, then, were derived from a study of the medieval political structure. This is still the place to turn, for, as we shall see, it is here, and here alone, that we find the sharply defined characteristics which make it possible to distinguish feudalism from other patterns of social organization. Some other societies had some of these characteristics, and one other society, Japan from 1300 to 1600, had most of them. But feudalism appeared first and developed most completely in Western Europe between 800 and 1200.

Definition of Feudalism. When we look at the political situation in Western Europe in this period, there are three things that strike us. First, there is a fragmentation of political power. Over much of Western Europe the county is the largest effective political unit, and in some places even the county has splintered into small, autonomous lordships. Moreover, even in these small districts no single ruler has a monopoly of political authority. There are rights of jurisdiction and administration which are held as hereditary possessions by lesser lords. There may be enclaves within a county or a barony in which the count or baron has no authority at all.

Second, this fragmented political power is treated as a private possession. It can be divided among heirs, given as marriage portion, mortgaged, bought and sold. Private contracts and the rules of family law determine the possessors of judicial and administrative authority. Public power in private hands is accepted as a normal and inevitable arrangement; no one considers it peculiar or undesirable.

[1] The medieval Latin word for fief was *feodum* or *feudum* —hence the French *féodalité* (which came first) and the slightly later English "feudalism."

Third, a key element in the armed forces—heavy-armed cavalry—is secured through individual and private agreements. Knights render military service not because they are citizens of a state or subjects of a king, but because they or their ancestors have promised to give this service to a lord in return for certain benefits. These benefits may range from mere sustenance in the lord's household to the grant of estates, villages, and even some rights of government. Increasingly, the grant of land comes to be the normal way of securing the services of a knight, but other arrangements are always possible. The essential point is that military service is provided through a series of private contracts between the lord and his men.

To sum up, the basic characteristics of feudalism in Western Europe are a fragmentation of political authority, public power in private hands, and a military system in which an essential part of the armed forces is secured through private contracts. Feudalism is a method of government, and a way of securing the forces necessary to preserve that method of government.

This is not as narrow a definition as it seems. The possessors of political and military power will naturally mold their society to fit their own needs. They will manipulate the economy so that they get the greatest share of production; they will develop a class structure which gives them the highest position; they will, as wealthy consumers, influence writers and artists; they will establish standards to which their society must conform. Thus, it is perfectly legitimate to speak of feudal society, or a feudal age, if we remember that it was the political-military structure which made the society and the age feudal.

On the other hand, if we try a wider definition, feudalism becomes an amorphous term. The most usual attempt to broaden the definition of feudalism stresses social and economic factors; in its simplest form it would find the essence of feudalism in the exploitation of an agricultural population by a ruling group. That this occurred in the feudal society of Western Europe is certainly true; it is equally true that it occurred in many other societies as well, both before and after the Middle Ages. Nor can we say that this situation is typical of all pre-industrial societies, and that therefore the socioeconomic definition of feudalism is useful in marking a universal stage of economic development. Some pre-industrial societies were never feudal in any sense of the word; some highly industrialized societies can be called feudal if we use the socioeconomic definition of feudalism. The ruling class (or party) of the Soviet Union built up its heavy industries by exploiting the tillers of the soil, and the ruling class of Communist China has recently attempted to do the same thing. A definition which can include societies as disparate as those of the Ancient Middle East, the late Roman Empire, medieval Europe, the southern part of the United States in the nineteenth century, and the Soviet Union in the 1930's is not much use in historical analysis.

— 2 —

ARMED RETAINERS OF THE PERIOD OF MIGRATIONS

Feudalism, then, is a set of political-military arrangements which existed in Western Europe in the Middle Ages. These arrangements began to take shape in the eighth century, but they obviously must have had roots in an earlier period. When we look for these roots, we find that the political and the military aspects of feudalism had different origins and different rates of growth. While the two aspects were associated quite early with each other, they were not fully meshed together for several centuries. Thus, the first stages of military feudalism and of political feudalism must be discussed separately.

Retainers in the Late Roman Empire. The armed retainer, the man who fights because he has a personal allegiance to a military leader, is a familiar figure both in the late Roman Empire and in the Germanic kingdoms with which the Empire had to deal. Roman armies of the fourth and fifth centuries had long ceased to be Roman. They were composed largely of barbarian contingents whose zeal and loyalty fluctuated alarmingly, and who were especially unreliable when they thought that they were on the losing side. Any sensible general wanted a bodyguard of his own men—elite troops who could be relied on to deliver a charge in a wavering battle or to cover a retreat. Civilian officials, and even wealthy private citizens, also wanted groups of private soldiers for protection in a period of disorder. These groups were often very large—a bodyguard of several thousand men was not unusual—and they were recruited from the lower classes. Many of them were slaves or barbarians. (*See Reading No. 2.*) Members of a bodyguard had some chance to become officers, but as long as they were simple soldiers there was nothing particularly honorable about their calling. They were more like a special class of servants than anything else. If they served their master faithfully they received food, clothing, a little pay, and, at times, a share of the spoils of war. But as a class they had no social standing and no political influence.

Retainers Among the Early Germans. The Germanic retainer appears earlier than the Roman and has a far higher social position. As early as the first century A.D. Tacitus describes a German institution he calls the *comitatus*—a band composed of young men of good family who have sought out a famous war-leader, and have pledged unswerving loyalty to him. (*See Reading No. 1.*) No leader has very many of these men, and he usually treats them with distinction. They are his companions rather than his servants; they receive presents rather than wages. If the leader is killed in battle and they survive, they are disgraced. On the other hand, if they win a series of victories, some of the companions will become leaders of war-bands in their turn, while others will return home and become local chieftains. They are, or can easily become, an aristocracy. Far fewer in number than their Roman counterparts, they have far greater influence.

There was certainly some connection between the two types of retainership. Most generals of the Late Empire were of Germanic origin; they may have introduced the idea of the *comitatus* into the Roman army while modifying it to meet Roman social conditions. Young Romans of good family were usually not eager to serve a barbarian commander. The emperors were quite satisfied with this situation, since young men of good family with military reputations were potential threats to the throne. Retainers, therefore, had to be found in the lower classes, and this meant in turn that they could not be given a distinguished status. On the whole, it made little difference that the member of a German *comitatus* was an aristocrat and the member of a Roman private army was not. Overriding all these social distinctions was the fact that in both Roman and German armies, the best and most reliable troops were the commander's personal retainers.

— 3 —

ARMED RETAINERS OF THE GERMANIC KINGDOMS

The importance of personal retainers was not forgotten in the next two centuries when Germanic kings gradually took over all the western part of the Roman Empire. Every king had his armed retainers, who were usually considered superior to other troops. The status of these retainers seems to have varied directly with the degree of Roman influence in their kingdoms. Thus in England, where Roman traditions had been almost blotted out, the retainers hold an honorable position and rapidly become an aristocracy. In the kingdom of the Franks, where Roman culture had left an indelible mark, the retainers are, at first, of lower rank. They are sometimes called *pueri regis,* "the king's boys," in exactly the same way in which servants were addressed as "boy!" in European colonies. And even the Celtic word *vassus,* or vassal, which gradually becomes the official designation of the retainer group, originally has much the same meaning—a young serving-man. Some of these early Frankish retainers had been slaves; many of them were of low birth, and it is not always easy to distinguish them from mere household servants.

Rise in the Status of Retainers. The status of the Frankish retainer, however, improved steadily in the seventh and eighth centuries. This improvement was due, in part, to the extreme simplicity of Germanic government. The Roman administrative system had collapsed long ago, and as far as there was any central government it was located in the royal household. No distinction was made between public and private services. The keeper of the king's horses or the keeper of the king's chamber could also be a member of the small group with whom the king took daily counsel. The armed retainer did not rise so high, but he did benefit from his position as a member of the household. (*See Reading No. 4.*)

Importance of Heavy Cavalry. Equally important were the changes in the art of war which made the heavy-armed horseman the dominant figure in European armies. The key innovation was probably the introduction of the stirrup from Asia to Western Europe. Without stirrups, cavalry had been almost useless for prolonged combat. Larger and stronger horses were also essential to carry a soldier in heavy armor, and this type of horse appeared for the first time after the collapse of the Roman Empire. In any case, by the middle of the eighth century Frankish leaders had found that mounted men wearing some kind of armor could defeat almost any other kind of troops. Quite naturally, they wanted their household soldiers to adopt this new mode of fighting.

Some problems arose, however. Armor was still relatively simple, but even a simple chain-mail shirt had to be made by hand. This was a slow and expensive process. Horses which could carry armed men were also expensive, and they had to be well fed. Any vigorous man could learn to be a passable foot-soldier with a little training, but fighting in armor on horseback required a great deal more drill. Soon it was being said that unless a man had started his training as a boy, he would never make a good mounted soldier.

Vassals. Men who used expensive equipment, who required years of special training, who formed an elite group in the army, gradually began to stand out from the mass of household servants. In an age of weak government and little economic opportunity, most men needed a local protector or lord, and we have documents which show how a man subjected himself to a lord—"commended himself," to use the technical phrase. In early documents of the seventh century it is rather difficult to know what services a "commended" man is expected to perform. He may be a fighter; he may be an attendant in the household; he may be both. (*See Reading No. 3.*) But by the end of the eighth century, the man who is a specialist in the new type of warfare is clearly distinguished from other retainers. He gains a virtual monopoly of the appellation *vassus* or *vassalus.* He will soon have a virtual monopoly of the word *miles. Miles* to a Roman meant a soldier of any sort. To a man of the Middle Ages it means primarily a heavy-armed cavalryman; it becomes the Latin equivalent for the English word "knight" or the French word "chevalier." And while it will be some centuries before a vassal or a knight is automatically considered a member of the aristocracy, even in the year 800 he clearly has a more honorable and influential position than the armed retainers of the Late Empire or early Frankish kingdom.

— 4 —

THE ORIGIN OF FIEFS

The expense of equipping and maintaining groups of heavy-armed cavalrymen led rapidly to another change in the status of this class. Money was scarce in early medieval Europe, while land was cheap and plentiful. Naturally enough, men who possessed large amounts of land began to consider using it to support their vassals. A vassal who had an estate, worked by a group of peasants, could take care of his own needs at no expense to the lord. At the same time, in return for the estate, he would continue to give military service to his superior.

Dependent Land Tenure. These arrangements were easy to envision because they fitted into an already existing pattern. Just as the lords had large numbers of men under their protection, from whom the vassals were only gradually distinguished, so they had large amounts of land under their protection. This happened in two ways. First, in a period of subsistence economy and rudimentary administrative systems, the easiest way to make some profit out of land ownership was to lend it or lease it to dependents. (*See Reading No. 5.*) In return the dependents gave payments in kind, or services, or both. Second, in an age of violence, small free landholders often found that they could not protect their property without the assistance of powerful men. They would surrender their land to a lord, and receive it back as tenants. (*See Reading No. 6.*) The lord would give them protection; they would give him rents and services of various kinds. In all these agreements, title to the land remained with the lord. Leases were at first not hereditary. Theoretically, they had to be renewed whenever the lord or tenant died. Failure to pay rent or to give service could lead to eviction, or at least to a reduction in the size of the holding. But, on the whole, these relationships had a tendency to become permanent and hereditary. The lord gained an assured income and the tenant had an assured livelihood, meager though it might be in some cases.

Precaria and Fiefs. Thus, to lend land to a retainer in return for service was nothing very new, and it was some time before the estates given to vassals acquired a special name. They were called at first *precaria,* which meant that they were granted as a favor and not as hereditary possessions. Then they were called *benefices* (*see Readings Nos. 11 and 12*), a word which still implied a favor, and which was not restricted to grants of land in return for military service. (For example, an office in the Church which brought in a steady income was also called a benefice.) Only around 1100 did the word *feudum* or fief come into common usage as a term to describe lands granted to a vassal.

This slow development of the nomenclature corresponded to the slow development of the institution. The first clear examples of the grant of a *precaria* to a military retainer come in the decades after 740 A.D. (*See Reading No. 7.*) This was a difficult period for the Frankish kingdom; it had to face assaults from Moslems coming up from the South and from unconverted Germans in the East. The emergency was so great that the kings even seized land from the church and granted it as *precaria* to their soldiers. Although many vassals received grants of land at this time, there were quite important vassals in the ninth century who had no estates at all (*see Reading No. 11*), and there never was a time when every military dependent was a landholder.

Gradual Spread of the Custom of Granting Fiefs. This delay in granting landed estates to vassals was caused by the fact that the operation involved disadvantages as well as advantages. What the lord saved in the expense of equipping and maintaining a soldier, he might lose in the amount of service rendered. A vassal who lived in the lord's household was always and immediately available for duty. This could not be true of a man living on his own estate. He had to have time for his own affairs; he had to be given some advance warning before he could be called to arms. Some lords, notably in Burgundy, tried to avoid these inconveniences by giving their vassals only small holdings grouped around a fortified post. The vassal had his own home and a small income, but he remained close to and dependent on his lord. Other lords gave estates only to their older and more experienced vassals, while younger men continued to live in the household. Landless knights were still quite common in the eleventh century, and they never entirely disappeared.

Nevertheless, the social and economic situation was such that, in the end, most vassals received grants of land. There was a shortage of manpower, and especially of trained manpower, throughout northern Europe. A lord who did not bind his vassals to him by grants of land found it hard to retain their loyalty, and even harder to replace them when they died. A vassal who had land was less likely to desert, and he would probably have a son eager to take his place when he died. Armor became more complete, more effective, and more expensive, so that the economic reason for granting land to vassals was strengthened. By 1100—earlier in some places—opinion had crystallized: a vassal was normally expected to have a fief.

— 5 —

STATUS OF KNIGHTS AND LESSER VASSALS

The Problem of Inheritance. Thus ended the first stage of the development of the military side of feudalism. The ordinary vassal, or knight, had improved his position markedly, but he was still subject to disabilities which would have shocked his thirteenth-century descendants. For example, the precarious nature of his tenure of his lands was emphasized in many ways. (*See Reading No. 12.*) The lord might seize his estates on flimsy excuses, or force him to exchange them for other, less desirable holdings. The knight could not be sure that his lands would go to his heirs, since when he died they legally reverted to the lord. If the knight left a son who by age and training was ready for military service, it was almost certain that the fief would be regranted to him. Even then, however, the son might not receive exactly the same holding which had been granted to his father. If the heir were a minor, a daughter, or a collateral relative, the lord might ignore his claims altogether. The best that could be hoped for would be that the lord would recognize the rights of these weaker claimants in return for additional payments. He might take the revenues of the land until the minor heir came of age (right of wardship); he might allow the daughter to inherit only if she married a man of his choice (right of marriage). As for collateral heirs, they might have to pay a heavy sum to have their claims recognized, or surrender part of the holding.

It is not surprising that vassals came to be obsessed with the problem of strengthening their hereditary rights in their estates, and that they were ready to support any political or legal innovations which would change the precarious possession of fiefs into something more like ownership. There is an echo of these feelings in the epic poems written for the feudal class in the twelfth century. In case after case the whole plot turns on the attempt of a lord to deprive a vassal of his rightful inheritance, and the vassal's struggle to retain it. (*See Reading No. 40.*)

Low Social Status of Knights. The weakness of the economic position of the lesser vassals was paralleled by their political weakness and relatively low social status. It is true that even in the ninth and tenth centuries, knights were infinitely better off than the great mass of the population. As expert fighting men they could expect to be better fed, better housed, and treated with more consideration than peasants. Nevertheless, the line between knight and peasant was not very sharply drawn in the first period of feudalism. A poor knight might be no wealthier than a rich peasant. Each might hold the same amount of land, and if the knight had serfs to work his land for him, the well-to-do peasant could hire poor laborers at very low rates of pay. In the confused period of the break-up of the Carolingian Empire, sons of peasants who were physically fit and of an adventurous spirit often became knights. Lords who needed soldiers did not worry about their social origins, and a peasant who proved to be a good cavalryman could pass his occupation on to his son. Serfs who served as knights remained common in Eastern France and Germany clear into the thirteenth century. (*See Reading No. 28.*) No one in 1100 would have thought that the knightly class as a whole was noble or aristocratic. Some knights were of noble descent, some were not, but as a class they were simply a group of specially trained and specially rewarded retainers. They could be given by one lord to another, just as any other dependents could be given. For example, an eleventh-century Norman duke gave a monastery a village with its peasants, mills, meadows, and knights. (*See Reading No. 21.*) It is only when the knight ceases to be primarily a soldier that he becomes a gentleman.

Political Weakness of Knights. Moreover, the individual knight had little political power. He could not be the ruler of a virtually independent district, as a great lord could, because he lacked the necessary military resources —castles and his own band of armed men. No mere knight could afford to build a strongly fortified place or recruit a group of warriors—at least not in the first period of feudalism. Being defenseless, he had to be dependent on a lord. The lord's castle was his refuge, and the lord's army, made up of his fellow-knights, was his protection.

In these circumstances, the knight could not expect to have extensive rights of government. Even if he were of good birth and had acquired or inherited fairly large landholdings, the most that he could expect was a sort of police-court jurisdiction over his peasants. He could settle minor squabbles—fights among villagers, disputes over peasant holdings or labor services—but any serious matters would go to the court of a superior. No knight would have jurisdiction in cases which involved heavy fines, or the death penalty; no knight would hear law-suits in which free men were disputing among themselves the possession of land. And many knights, probably the majority, had no rights of justice of any kind.

Knights and the Lords' Courts. In the long run, the knightly class gained its greatest political influence by participating in the administrative and judicial work of the courts of the lords. But it took some time to reach even this modest level of power. As we shall see, the lords were at first primarily public officials, and they ruled over many men who were not their vassals. Even in the most thoroughly feudalized parts of Europe it took two or three centuries before most owners of large estates put their land under a lord's protection and became his vassals. In many places (southern France, for example), this process never reached completion, and large numbers of landowners remained outside of the lord-vassal relationship.

The old tradition, going back to the early Germanic kingdoms, was that these independent landowners were the natural assistants of the local governor, and this tradition continued when the local governor became a feudal lord. A knight with a small fief was by no means the equal of a man whose family had long owned sizable properties. So the lords at first used the old landowning group in their courts and in their administration, or turned to members of their own families or members of the clergy for assistance. (*See Reading No. 17.*) It was only very gradually, as the great-estate owners became guardians of castles, and then more or less independent rulers, that knights were introduced into the courts and councils of their lords. Castle-holders were either too busy or too important to come to the old courts of the count and viscount, so knights were invited to take their places. (*See Readings Nos. 18 and 19.*) It was unthinkable for a lord to hold court by himself. It was politically unwise to assume full responsibility, and socially degrading not to be surrounded by respectful subordinates. If a court could not be filled except by inviting knights, then knights had to be used.

This transition took place largely in the late tenth and early eleventh centuries. After 1000 even the king of France found that he had to summon knights to replace the counts and barons who had formerly made up his court. By 1100 the knights have become an essential group in most feudal courts; the lord regularly asks their advice, or at least notifies them when he is making an important decision. In judicial matters, the theory is developing that the lord should not be a judge in cases involving his own interests, and that therefore he merely presides over the court, while the knights and other vassals render the judgment. But we should not exaggerate the power of the knights in these situations. The lord may ask advice, but he does not have to take it, and the knights very seldom give a judgment which is displeasing to their superior. The chief gain which they derive from this involvement in administrative and judicial work is that they are ceasing to be mere soldiers, and are being trained to be a governing class.

— 6 —

KINGS AND COUNTS

Limits of the Military Usefulness of Feudalism. The development of the armed retainer into the knight explains the military aspect of feudalism, but it does not explain feudalism as a method of political organization. The specially trained and specially privileged fighting man has existed in many nonfeudal societies—for example, the Ottoman Empire. Granted that the heavy-armed cavalry-man of tenth-century Europe was an outstanding example of the elite soldier, he was not important enough in himself to create a new type of government. It is doubtful that any ruler of any importance ever depended entirely upon the services of his knights for his military operations, or that any important battle was ever decided simply by a clash between knights of the two opposing leaders. Feudal arrangements were a convenient way of raising an important element of an army, but they were not the only way of raising an army. Infantry and light-armed cavalry had some value, even in the period when the heavy-armed knight reached the peak of his military efficiency. Rulers continued to require military service of all free men (most of whom were not knights), especially for defense. They also continued to recruit soldiers of all types without making them knights, either by promising them a share in the spoils of war, or by paying them wages for a single campaign. To take the most famous example, William's army at Hastings was recruited from all over northern France and included bowmen and other foot-soldiers. These men had owed no service to William before; they joined his army because he promised them a share of the spoils. William could never have conquered England if he had depended only on the military service furnished by knights of his duchy of Normandy.

In short, if feudalism had been simply a method of raising specially trained and equipped soldiers, it would have been a most unsuccessful experiment. The period during which knights rendered significant military service in return for fiefs was a relatively brief one. On the one hand, we have seen that the practice of granting fiefs to vassals developed and spread quite slowly; it was not much before the year 900 that it could be assumed that the great majority of vassals had fiefs. On the other hand, as soon as large numbers of vassals held fiefs, they began to strive to reduce the amount of military service which they owed. This development will be discussed in more detail in a later section, but it was already having serious effects by 1100. Thus, if we look only at the military side, we should have to conclude that feudalism was hardly worth studying. Even at its peak, it never furnished enough soldiers for major military operations, and after 1100 it became increasingly useless as a way of providing any military service at all.

Feudalism, however, had a political as well as a military side, and it was the political side of feudalism which had an enduring effect upon Western European history. Every institution of the early modern state grew out of or was modified by the political aspects of feudalism. Our government bureaus, our courts and codes of law, our representative assemblies, our ideas of constitutionalism, all bear the mark of their feudal origins.

Power and Position of the Count. To understand this, we must go back again to the fact that the Germanic kingdoms which succeeded the Roman Empire had almost no political organization. The king and his companions dealt with affairs as they arose; there were no specialized administrative departments, no hierarchy of officials, no regular connections between the king's court and scattered local communities. This system worked well enough when kingdoms were small, but as they grew, some kind of administrative structure was required. The Roman model was available, but could not be used, partly because few kings understood it, partly because of a lack of money and of trained men, partly because the people of Western Europe had become rather weary of the elaborate and expensive Roman administrative apparatus. Instead of trying to preserve the Roman system, a simpler administrative pattern was developed. The kingdom was divided into districts, and a representative of the king (usually called a count) was chosen to administer each district. The counts ruled their districts very much as the king ruled his kingdom. They had full military, judicial, and financial power, which they exercised with the aid of their household companions and the advice of the leading landholders of the district. Thus, the administrative problem was solved by breaking the kingdom into what were in effect subkingdoms—districts small enough to be governed by simple procedures. (*See Reading No. 13.*) As long as a count kept the king's confidence, he was subject to very little control from the center.

The danger, of course, was that the counts would become virtually independent rulers. With very few exceptions, the counts were chosen from great noble families—families strong enough to cause the king a good deal of trouble if he offended one of their members. Many counts remained in the same district all their lives, and so were able to build up strong groups of local supporters. Supervision of the count's activities was loose and intermittent. There were general regulations, applicable to all counts, which encouraged them to do their duty and forbade them to abuse their power. These regulations were often admirably worded, but they were hard to enforce. The king, as he moved about his realm from one royal estate to another, would investigate the acts of some of his counts, and he might send out agents to give orders to or hear complaints against others. But only the strongest kings, such as Charlemagne, did this regularly, and even the strong kings found it difficult to follow up all the reports they received. Very few counts ever lost their positions for official misconduct.

Checks on the Power of the Count. By and large, administrative regulations for keeping counts under control were not very effective. Certain political devices gave better results. In the first place, the king could weaken the counts by establishing rival authorities in each county.

At a very early date most religious establishments—monasteries and bishoprics—received grants of immunity. This meant that they were placed under direct royal protection. Counts and their subordinates were forbidden to enter the territory of an immunity, either to perform acts of justice or to collect money. (*See Reading No. 9.*) The bishops or abbots in effect were placed on the same level as the count; they ruled their districts under very loose supervision from the king. Somewhat later, but before 800, immunities were granted to certain laymen (*see Reading No. 10*), and these men also became independent of the count. The count could request the cooperation of men who held immunities, but he could not force them to obey him.

Another counterbalance to the power of the count was created when, around the year 800, the kings began to settle some of their most favored vassals on estates scattered through various parts of the kingdom. These *vassi dominici* (vassals of the lord king) were supposed to aid the counts, but their first loyalty was to the king; the count could not expect unswerving obedience from them. (*See Reading No. 11.*) And all these people, prelates, great lay landlords, and royal vassals, had direct access to the king. They could bring their grievances to his court; they could start dangerous intrigues against a count who had offended them.

In fact, intrigue at the royal court was the second political factor which kept counts from becoming too independent. There were always factions among the king's favorites and advisers. These men were drawn largely from the great families of the realm, and the representatives of each family sought power and offices for their members and allies. Some kings seem to have favored first one family and then another in a deliberate attempt to keep any subordinate from establishing a permanent basis of power. Thus, it behooved a count to stand well with the faction which was dominant at the moment, and this in turn meant that he had to pay some attention to the wishes of the central government. If he ignored or displeased the political leaders of the court, he could easily lose his position; if he stood well with them, he might be promoted.

The Great Commands. For there were positions which gave more wealth and power than a countship—the great commands set up to protect frontier areas. One of these great commands might include a dozen or more counties. The man who held it was incomparably more powerful than an ordinary count. He usually had the special title of duke or marquis; he could appoint large numbers of subordinate officials; he could make policy for a very wide area. These great commands were the real prizes of court intrigue. They were what the ambitious heads of great families desired above everything else. But to obtain them, one had to please both the king and his favorites of the moment, which meant carrying out the broad line of policy laid down by the court.

The result of all these factors was that while the great families held all the important positions, they did not, for many generations, take root in specific districts. There was a certain amount of movement caused by the rise and fall of factions at court, and by the desires of the aristocrats themselves. In the early Middle Ages, there was no rule of primogeniture and no preference for descendants through the male line. Thus, while there was a tendency to give counties only to men who had some tie of kinship with previous counts, there could easily be a dozen or so candidates who had such ties. Conversely, a young man of good family might be connected with counts in a dozen counties. In deciding which county he was to have, much would depend on the wishes of his own family or that of his wife's, and on the degree of influence which either family had at court. Appointments to the great commands were even more flexible, because at first they were not expected to be permanent. To take the most famous example, the earliest known ancestor of the Capetian dynasty was probably a count in the Rhineland. He was sent to western France to guard the region between the Loire and the Seine against attacks by the Bretons. But when he died in 866, he was replaced by a man of quite a different family. In short, as late as the ninth century no family could claim permanent, hereditary possession of any great office. (*See Reading No. 14.*)

This system, however, could not last if the king's power sank below a certain minimum level. He had to be able to displace counts, even if he did it only occasionally. He had to have some freedom in alloting the great commands. He had to preserve a situation in which more could be gained by seeking the king's favor than by trying to establish an independent local base of power.

— 7 —

THE RISE OF FEUDAL PRINCIPALITIES

Decline of Royal Power. During the late ninth and tenth centuries the political balance began to swing against the kings. Germanic rulers often divided their kingdoms among their sons, and the sons were seldom pleased with the terms of the divisions. This discontent often led to civil war, and civil war, in turn, weakened royal powers of appointment and dismissal. A count threatened with loss of office could always counter with a threat to join the king's rival.

Division among sons and the ensuing civil wars also had a tendency to split big kingdoms into smaller ones. This meant that the king had less to give, and that there were fewer choices for young men of good family. The eldest son of a count began to insist that he should inherit his father's county, because there was often nothing else which he could claim. (*See Reading No. 16.*) Finally, a series of invasions—by Northmen, Saracens, Magyars—threw greater burdens on local authorities and discredited central governments. It was seldom that a king could get together an army in time to strike a band of these swift-moving raiders. The local duke or count had to take responsibility for defense. Naturally enough, he began to feel that the land he had defended was his own. Naturally enough, also, the people he had defended began to think of him as their real ruler instead of the distant king.

All Western Europe was affected by these developments, but they hit France first and hardest. Civil war and the raids of the Northmen did more damage in France than elsewhere, and royal power declined more rapidly in France than in England or Germany. It was in France that the great families first began to take root in specific districts. With less and less to gain from the king, it became more and more important to establish a strong local basis of power. During the tenth century, French counts and dukes established hereditary, autonomous principalities.

Origin of French Principalities. These principalities did not all originate in the same way. The clearest example of a great command which turned directly into a principality was the duchy of Burgundy, established to guard the frontier against the kingdom of Arles. (Arles, by the way, was a great command which had earlier become entirely independent.) The duchy of Aquitaine, when it reached its final form, represented the uniting of two great commands which had been created to hold down the turbulent southwest. Normandy represented the failure of a great command. The Vikings had occupied all the counties of the lower Seine and the western coast as far as Brittany; their leader had to be recognized as duke of what had once been a part of the northern frontier command. Flanders may have had a tenuous connection with an old northeast frontier command, but it owed its existence primarily to the skill and energy of its counts, who had united, by marriage, diplomacy, or conquest, many small counties. The Blois-Champagne complex of counties was a similar case. Finally, Anjou is typical of the principalities which grew out of the splitting up of great commands. The Angevin counts were at one time merely viscounts, deputies of the Robertian dukes who held the great command between the Loire and the Seine. But as the Robertians began to covet the throne itself, they had little time for local affairs and had to allow their viscounts more freedom. The viscount of Angers became count of Anjou and the dominant power on the lower Loire. However their power was acquired, the great lords of France were alike in two respects—they gave the king only such assistance as they desired, and they ignored him completely in the internal administration of their lands.

— 8 —

FEUDAL FRAGMENTATION AT ITS HEIGHT

In France, by the year 1000, one of the chief ingredients of feudalism—public power in private hands—was firmly established. By that date, another element of feudalism—vassalage and the fief—was also well developed. But the connections between these two aspects of feudalism were still loose, and it was by no means inevitable that they should become closer. Hereditary principalities can exist without vasals; strong central governments have often found vassals (or at least an hereditary military class) useful. It took about a century to combine the military and political aspects of feudalism, and once again, the combination came first, and was most complete, in northern France.

Oaths of Loyalty and Hereditary Offices. The process began when the kings realized that they were losing control of their great officials. They tried to bind them more closely by personal oaths, and the strongest and most effective oath they knew was that of the vassal to his lord. Thus counts, dukes, and for that matter, many bishops took oaths to their kings which were very much like those of vassals. (*See Readings Nos. 8, 15, and 26.*) There has been a long and rather unprofitable argument as to whether the great men who took such oaths should be called vassals. Ninth- and tenth-century writers seldom applied the word to important men; they usually called them *fideles*—that is, men who had promised to be faithful to their superior. Even if a count occasionally was called a vassal, this use of the word is almost meaningless. A count was almost as far above an ordinary vassal as he was above a serf. The count was noble, had great political authority, and could maintain his independence against anyone—even at times against the king. The ordinary vassal was not noble, had no power of his own, and, in fact, was helpless except as a member of the military household of a great man. Similarity of oath does not mean similarity of status.

What was important was that the king could no longer depend on his public authority; he had to establish a private and personal bond between himself and his officials. This was the first step toward basing political power on private arrangements. The next step was to begin treating the office of count or duke as a fief. This happened when the distinction between the office, which gave political power, and lands connected with the office, which gave the office-holder his income, was blurred—when kings in bestowing countships spoke of giving "benefices" to their faithful men, when hereditary possession of high offices received at least *de facto* recognition. (*See Reading No. 16.*) But here again, the distinction between the great men and ordinary military retainers must be made. In the early days of feudalism a county or a duchy was seldom if ever called a fief, and in many ways it was quite unlike the fief of a petty knight. A knight had land, but no political power; a count might have extensive political power in an area where he possessed no land. A knight owed quite definite services, especially military service, in return for his fief. A count owed fidelity, which at most implied only a vague obligation to be helpful, and often only a promise not to harm the superior. (*See Reading No. 22.*) A knight's fief was precarious in every sense of the word; the lord could confiscate it for very slight reasons. A count's holding could usually be seized only at the price of war, and he was more apt to lose it to an aggressive neighbor than to an aggrieved superior. Legally, the count and his county were becoming like the vassal and his fief, but in practice there was little resemblance between the two situations.

Growth of Subordinate Jurisdictions. This sharp distinction began to be blurred about the year 1000. The great men slowly lost their monopoly of political power, first to their immediate subordinates, then to even less important men. Most vassals (of whatever sort) acquired some judicial and administrative rights. In the end, there was an almost continuous spectrum of political authority from the village court of a petty knight to the high court of the territorial prince. It was this extreme fragmentation of political power which was the final stage in the development of feudalism. It was during the course of this fragmentation that the political and military aspects of feudalism merged to form a new and indissoluble whole.

Rudimentary as early medieval government was, the counts had not been able to govern entirely without assistance. They had deputies (viscounts and the like) who replaced them in their absence or who supervised subdistricts of their counties. As we have seen, both the count and his deputies were supposed to act (and especially to judge) with the advice of the leading men of the community (king's vassals and important landlords). (*See Readings Nos. 13, 17, 18, and 20.*) These deputies and advisers of the counts were obviously in the best position to acquire fragments of the counts' political power.

The process went very much as it had at the higher level. As the power of the kings weakened, the dukes and counts had to protect themselves both from their neighbors and from foreign raiders. They often had to leave local defenses and local administration in the hands of a viscount (or other subordinate) while they fought in remote parts of their lands. They had to build castles, or encourage their assistants to build them, in order to protect their subjects against sudden raids. And since the count could occupy only one or two castles with his own forces, the rest had to be entrusted to viscounts, *vassi dominici,* and heads of leading local families.

In this situation, political success could be almost as dangerous as military failure. For example, the Robertians (ancestors of the Capetian kings of France), after much difficulty, gained hereditary possession of the great command which included most of the counties between the Seine and the Loire. This was a great political success, but it immediately created military problems. The Robertians could not defend every part of this vast territory, especially as they were deeply involved in intrigues at the royal court. They had to give a very free hand to their deputies, and the abler or more fortunate deputies used this opportunity to become virtually independent. As we have seen, the viscount of Angers, originally only an agent of the Robertian duke, became count of Anjou and ancestor of the great Plantagenet family. Other viscounts also became counts, and when Hugh Capet seized the crown in 987, he retained direct control of only a few counties in the old family duchy. Much the same thing happened in the duchies of Burgundy and Aquitaine. The duke could keep his position only by allowing his subordinates a large degree of autonomy. As a result, the outlying counties of both duchies were lost, and the duke retained real power only in a small area.

On the other hand, a count or duke who was militarily weak saw his power disappear even more completely. If he could not protect his lands, they were either seized by a neighboring count, or his subjects turned to the nearest strong man—a viscount or the lord of a castle—for protection. This is what occurred in large parts of south central France. The first Bourbons, for example, were not even viscounts, but merely lords of a well-fortified castle.

War, brigandage, and the sheer difficulty of traveling over incredibly bad roads made most people prefer a nearby ruler to a distant one. Thus the county tended to disintegrate as a political unit. Over much of France, the working unit of government became the castellany—that is, the land near enough a castle so that it could be protected, policed, and administered by the lord of the castle. A district twenty miles long and twelve wide was a big castellany; many were smaller. The lord of a large castellany was in some areas practically independent of any higher authority.

Not all France suffered this extreme fragmentation. The duchy of Normandy, put together by a conquering line of dukes in the tenth century, never broke up into castellanies. The counties of Flanders and Anjou had castellanies, but they were closely controlled by the counts. Even where the castellans were most independent, there was some chance for the counts to influence their conduct. But in spite of these exceptions, it is still true that about the year 1100 most of the judicial, administrative and military business in France was conducted at the level of the castellany. (*See Readings Nos. 18 and 20.*)

Social and Political Rise of the Knights. Viscounts and castellans were descended from noble families, a lesser nobility than that of the countly families, but nevertheless recognized as noble. We can trace the origins of many viscounts on the Loire or Rhône back at least as far as that of the counts and dukes who were their masters. On the other hand, most knights, as we have seen, were not of noble families. But the difference between a knight who had a reasonably large fief, and the lord of a small castellany was not nearly so great as that between a knight and a count. Again, as the size of the effective political unit decreased, the importance of the knight increased. A public court of the age of Charlemagne, presided over by a count who might be a relative of the king and attended by the heads of the great local families of the province, was no place for low-born military retainers. But there were not many great families in a little castellany. A lord who wanted his court attended by leading men could often find no one better than his knights. (*See Reading No. 18.*) As we have seen, even the king of France, during the first half of the eleventh century, discovered that he could fill his courts only by inviting knights, and a knight who attended the court of a count or a castellan gained some of the political experience which he had hitherto lacked.

Thus some of the distinctions between the lesser nobility and the ordinary knights began to fade. If a castellan could have a court, a knight might be allowed to have one too. It would not be much of a court, to be sure; it would deal only with petty cases that were scarcely profitable enough to interest great men, but it was a court all the same. The holder of a court gained both authority and income. The threat of being summoned to a court was often enough to make humble men obedient to unjustified requests of the fief-holder. Conviction in a court almost always produced a profit to the court-holder. There was no nonsense about jail sentences, which would have been expensive. The guilty had to pay fines, or forfeit property if they could not pay. From being a household retainer, the knight had become a landlord; now, from being a landlord, he had become a judge with some powers of command. The process was not uniform. In some parts of France every holder of a fief had some rights of justice; in others there were fief-holders who had no judicial power. But by 1100 there were enough knights with powers of justice and enough knights attending the courts of their lords to assure a marked increase in their social position and their political importance.

Development of Feudalism in England and Germany. The process which we have been describing began earliest, and reached its fullest development, in northern and central France. During most of the eleventh century, England, Germany, southern France, and northern Italy lagged behind. Each in its own way preserved some aspects of the early Germanic kingdoms—the survival of public courts, the existence of important landholders who had not taken the feudal oath, the precarious position of the vassal, and the power of the king to reassign great commands (earldoms in England and dukedoms in Germany). (*See Reading No. 27.*) But these older political forms showed no great vitality. Fiefs may have been less important in southern France and northern Italy than they were between the Seine and the Loire, but political fragmentation was proceeding rapidly in both areas. To dispossess an English earl or a German duke usually meant civil war, as Edward the Confesser learned when he tried to deprive earl Godwin of his earldoms. In the last quarter of the eleventh century, when they met a real crisis, both the old English and old German kingdoms collapsed. The invasion of England by William of Normandy, and the rebellion inspired by the Investiture Conflict in Germany, showed the inadequacy of the old system. Both English and German institutions had to be reconstructed, and in the process they became more like those of northern France.

England, because it was a relatively small country, could be governed like one of the more cohesive French principalities. William divided the lands of the kingdom among his vassals, and he gave his vassals rights of justice over their retainers and peasants. But as suzerain of the Norman warriors and as heir of the Anglo-Saxon kings, he retained effective administrative control throughout the country. His sheriffs—the equivalents of the continental viscounts—had real authority in their counties, and in most of England certain serious criminal cases—murder, arson, rape—were reserved for the courts of the sheriff or the king. Even the greatest vassals had to give obedient service to William and his sons; if they failed in their duties, they were quickly punished. (*See Reading No. 24.*) Only in frontier districts, such as the Marches of Wales, did full political fragmentation take place. The Marcher Lords were more independent than any vassals in England proper, and their independence continued to plague the kings well into the fifteenth century.

In Germany, the growth of feudalism helped build up principalities not unlike those of tenth-century France. The great commands—duchies and margraviates—became hereditary possessions of certain families, and the men who held these positions rendered very little service to their nominal superior, the king. The kings attempted to reduce the power of the German dukes by using every opportunity to split off portions of their duchies. For example, the duchy of Austria was carved out of the great duchy of Bavaria in 1156 when there was a dispute over the succession. (*See Reading No. 48.*) But while such expedients helped a little, the princes of the German kingdom remained a very powerful group. They had more direct administrative authority than the king, and they controlled greater military forces. Eventually they became, to all intents and purposes, independent rulers.

By 1100, then, the fragmentation of political power, and the private possession of public authority, expressed in terms of the vassal and the fief, were dominant elements in the political structure of the key countries of Western Europe. The old type of Germanic kingdom was very nearly as dead as the Roman Empire. If real states were to be built in Western Europe, they would have to be constructed in large part out of feudal materials.

— 9 —

THE DEVELOPMENT OF STRONG FEUDAL STATES

The Least Fragmented Principalities: Normandy, Flanders, Anjou. The prospects for developing strong states out of feudal materials could not have looked very promising to an eleventh-century observer. As we have seen, the effective unit of government over much of Europe was the small district called the castellany. The castellany was an effective unit of government precisely because it did not need the full governmental machinery of a state. It was small enough so that one man, with a few assistants, could do all the work of government, small enough so that the ruler could know almost every house and the inhabitants of every house in his lands. Its strength was in personal loyalties, the loyalties of men who have known each other intimately for many years. Its weakness was the absence of institutions which could reach beyond and endure beyond the brief span of personal loyalties. A castellany had almost no political structure, no specialized political personnel. A man of exceptional ability might be able to rule two or three castellanies. Beyond that he would have to rely on deputies whose natural desire was to become autonomous castellans themselves. It seemed most unlikely that the political rubble of the castellanies could be solidified into the concrete of a state.

There were, as we have seen, a few regions where castellanies were not the dominant political unit. Castellanies had never existed in Normandy, except in the exposed zone which bordered on the lands of the French king. William, therefore, had no reason, and was under no pressure, to introduce them into England after the Conquest. Castellanies existed in Flanders, but were closely controlled by the count. In Anjou, the count also had more than the usual degree of control over his castellans. But in each of these three principalities there were special reasons for the absence or weakness of castellanies. Anjou was at first a relatively small county. A vigorous count could easily maintain personal contacts with all important men and keep castle-holders from becoming too independent. In Flanders, there were remarkably few families of the lesser nobility, and the count was already beginning to profit from the wealth of the textile-manufacturing cities. Except in times of disputed succession to the county, the Flemish castellans remained very much under the count's control. Normandy, created by a Viking conquest, was a new and abnormal principality. It had scarcely begun to take shape before the last half of the tenth century. The old governing families had been driven out, and the new ones had scarcely had time to take root. The first dukes had a free hand to organize their province as they desired, and they seem deliberately to have avoided some of the weaknesses of neighboring areas. For example, it was only in Normandy that viscounts remained public officials, accountable to the duke. England after 1066 had much the same experience as Normandy. The old Anglo-Saxon aristocracy was eradicated, and the new Norman aristocracy could have only the power which a victorious king was willing to grant.

Few other regions could expect the combination of favorable circumstances and able leadership which had prevented excessive political fragmentation in Anjou, Flanders, Normandy, and England. And even in these favored states, tendencies toward fragmentation were strong, and at times almost irresistible. Weak rulers like Robert Curthose of Normandy allowed local lords to gain power. Disputed successions, like those of Henry I (1100) and Stephen (1135) in England, forced successful claimants to buy the support of great men with sweeping concessions. It was not at all certain in 1100 that England and Normandy, Anjou and Flanders, would become the models for the development of centralized states. It was just as likely that their fate would resemble that of Germany, where the late advent of fragmentation only made its results more disastrous.

The Building of Feudal Systems. Yet, by 1200 it was clear that the tendency toward political fragmentation could be arrested, and even reversed, by techniques growing out of the feudalism of England and the North of France. The success of these techniques was aided, of course, by the economic revival and intellectual advances of the twelfth century. But where the new techniques of feudalism were not used (as in Italy) or were clumsily used (as in Germany), neither prosperity nor intellectual progress could prevent the continuing—even the worsening—of political fragmentation.

The first of these new techniques was the building of feudal institutions and customs into a system: that is, the establishment of a regular hierarchy among the possessors of political power and the invention of general rules governing relations among members of the hierarchy. Feudalism had existed for generations, but it became a system only in the twelfth century. And it is precisely because it was not a system before the twelfth century that it was so disorderly and amorphous. Old political units were breaking up; new ones were being formed; personal loyalties were being transferred from kings to counts and from counts to castellans. No one knew exactly what service a man owed his lord. Especially among great men, the feudal bond was often defined in negative terms, as merely an obligation not to do harm. (*See Reading No. 22.*) Nobody knew exactly what were the proper relations among lords, what powers and what lands each lord was supposed to possess. It was this confusion which caused so many of the petty wars of early feudalism, though it is only fair to add that the confusion also kept most feudal wars from being either very long or very bloody. Few men had enough resources, enough authority over their vassals, and enough confidence in their own cause, to carry on prolonged conflicts. It takes an organized state to wage a really violent war, and there were no organized states in the early days of feudalism.

The political fragmentation which reached its peak in the eleventh century had created a state of disorder and uncertainty which annoyed many people. The Church developed the idea of the Peace of God, a set of rules to protect noncombatants, such as peasants and merchants, from being attacked and plundered by warring lords. Intelligent rulers, such as the Duke of Normandy, seized upon this idea with joy. By helping the Church to enforce its rules they gained an opportunity for intervening in cases which otherwise might not have been in their jurisdiction. They also had an excuse for interfering in private wars, and for preventing any one of their vassals from becoming too strong through successful aggression against his neighbors. (*See Reading No. 25.*) The Peace Movement reached its peak with the First Crusade (1095), which had, among other objectives, that of removing the most belligerent warriors from Europe and sending them to fight in Syria. At this point the Peace Movement was reinforced by the revival of legal studies, which began in Italy shortly before 1100. Legal scholars naturally wanted greater precision in political structure and greater use of courts to settle disputes. Most rulers had scholars in their service (if only to write letters to the pope) who could be formidably legalistic when they wished. But even more important than the exhortations of the Church and the influence of scholars were the cold facts of the political situation. An ambitious ruler who wanted to increase his power and territories, and to hand them over unimpaired to his son, found that he had to create some sort of a system, some kind of permanent institutions, to preserve his gains. Military victory without political organization was fruitless. When the king of France conquered Burgundy in a long war which began in 1002, he could not keep it. When William conquered England in 1066, he not only kept it, but made it the strongest state in Western Europe. He did this by developing certain ideas which were latent in feudalism as it was practiced in the eleventh century. Other rulers, trying to increase their power, did much the same things, and so feudal systems were created.

The Theory of Delegated Powers. The most important idea which developed out of the confusion of early feudalism was the idea that all political power was delegated from a higher to a lower lord. God gave the king his realm with full powers; the king then gave a county to a count with wide powers (but not independence); the count gave out baronies with lesser powers; the barons gave their knights fiefs with police-court justice. (*See Reading No. 31.*) Any subordinate who abused his power could be punished by his immediate superior: thus, a baron who exceeded his authority or denied a subject justice could be punished by the count from whom he held his barony.

Needless to say, this concept of the delegation of political power represented neither historical experience nor actual practice. The political power of a count (or a baron) had depended much more on his own efforts and those of his ancestors than on authority specifically delegated by some superior in the remote past. And almost everywhere there were sharp breaks in the chain of command which supposedly ran from the king to the knight. Sometimes the break came between king and count, sometimes between count and castellan (or viscount), sometimes at both places. The king of France could not interfere in any way with the administration of the duchy of Normandy, but the duke of Normandy could and did control the activities of his viscounts and barons. The count of Toulouse was virtually independent of the king, but his viscounts were very nearly as independent of him.

Nevertheless, the concept of delegated power had real value. It justified powers which some of the greater lords were already exerting; it prepared the way for the rapid growth of new powers. It would have been ridiculous if the king of France had cited William the Conqueror to the royal court because William had not done justice to one of his vassals. It was not ridiculous, but a highly effective political move, when a king of France summoned William's great-great-grandson, John, for precisely this fault. (*See Reading No. 34.*) In the late eleventh century there were lords of castles in Aquitaine or in Burgundy who held their lands in full property; they were not even in theory vassals of their dukes. By the thirteenth century most of these lords had been persuaded or pressured into becoming vassals and were reasonably obedient to the orders of their dukes. (*See Reading No. 52.*) This same consolidation of power through emphasis on feudal subordination was taking place in many French principalities and in some German principalities during the twelfth century.

Protection of Rear-Vassals. Another advantage which resulted from the concept of delegated powers was that it allowed powerful rulers to deal directly with lesser vassals and freemen instead of passing through the tedious and often tenuous chain of feudal command. This may seem to contradict what has just been said about the importance of keeping the chain intact; actually it is only the other side of the picture. The idea of delegated power implied that the delegator reserved some rights for himself. The realities of feudal politics demanded that the superior demonstrate his possession of these rights by exercising power in the lands of his subordinates. In this way, subjects could be reminded that the local lord was not all-powerful, and the local lord was prevented from building up his strength by oppressing landholders in his neighborhood.

The higher lord might make his presence felt in subordinate lordships in two ways. One was by reserving certain sorts of lawsuits for direct decision in his own courts. For example, Henry II of England reserved all suits dealing with feudal tenure for royal courts. (*See Reading No. 32.*) The other method was to allow the local lord to hear the case in the first instance, but to make it very easy to appeal from his decision to the court of the superior lord, and to take the person and property of the appellant under the direct protection of the superior. This second method developed later than the first, but by the end of the twelfth century it was becoming a potent weapon, and was especially favored by the kings of France. (*See Readings Nos. 33 and 34.*)

It is obvious that kings, dukes, and counts profited from the systematizing of feudalism. It may be less obvious that the other group which profited was the one at the very bottom of the feudal ladder—the lesser knights and rear-vassals.[1] These people were easily oppressed by their immediate lords: they might be forced to give too much service; they or their heirs might be deprived of their fiefs on various pretexts. Definition of feudal obligations and enforcement of these definitions in the courts of the superior lord were greatly to the interest of the lesser vassal. Almost always he gained greater security of tenure and a diminution of required services. This meant that rear-vassals were usually in favor of the centralizing tendencies of superior lords whether these tendencies were in full accord with earlier feudal customs or not.

This attitude, in turn, made it easier for the great lords to consolidate their power. After all, a castellan, or a viscount, depended largely on the services of his vassals; he had little money with which to hire mercenaries. If his vassals refused to serve him in rebellions or private wars, and if he could not punish them because they would be protected by the overlord, then the autonomy of the castellan was at an end.

The German Feudal System. The alliance of the superior lord with the rear-vassals against the intermediate lords was one of the most important developments of the twelfth century. It was most effective in England, where the barons lost all local political power (except in the Marches of Wales and Scotland). It became increasingly effective in France, especially after the French kings developed their system of appeals. In Germany, it worked only at the level of the principalities. Frederick Barbarossa, Holy Roman Emperor and king of Germany, saw the advantages of systematizing feudalism, but he was a little too systematic. This may have been because feudalism developed so late in Germany that Frederick could not, or did not, rely entirely on limited German experience and precedents, but instead showed some tendency to rely on English and French methods which

[1] A rear-vassal was, in simplest form, the vassal of a vassal. Of course, the chain might be longer. Thus, a knight of the lord of Tancarville who was a vassal of the duke of Normandy who was a vassal of the king of France was three degrees removed from his highest superior.

he did not fully understand. At any rate, while he insisted on a complete and logical feudal chain of command, he did not allow for the short cuts which put the kings of England, and eventually the kings of France, in direct contact with rear-vassals. Everything had to go through channels; the princes stood between the emperor and the lesser vassals. As a result, the state in Germany grew out of the principalities and not out of the German kingdom.

— 10 —

ECONOMIC ASPECTS OF THE FEUDAL RELATIONSHIP

Decrease in Personal Service. The building of feudal systems in the twelfth century was made easier by a growing tendency to stress the economic aspects of the feudal relationship. During the twelfth century both lords and vassals found it to their advantage to decrease the old emphasis on personal service. The vassals naturally wanted time to look after their own affairs; they tried to establish rules limiting the number of days of service at their own expense which could be required by their lords. Almost everywhere they succeeded in cutting service down to a few weeks; the most common limit was forty days. They also tried to establish the rule that services were not required outside certain boundaries. For example, English vassals argued that they did not have to fight in France. This effort was less successful than the attempt to limit the length of service, but it caused enough controversy so that no lord could be entirely sure that his vassals would follow him on a distant expedition.

As for the lords, they accepted these limitations because, by 1100, the ordinary vassal was not necessarily a very good soldier. As fiefs became hereditary, there was no assurance that the heir would have the physical qualities needed to make an effective fighting man. As vassals became absorbed in their work as landlords and minor judges, many of them spent little time in the training required for service as heavy-armed cavalry. In other cases fiefs had been subdivided [1] to a point where the service owed was useless—five days or ten days. (*See Reading No. 30.*) As we have seen, it is doubtful that at any time a lord could have relied entirely on the unpaid service of his vassals to produce a satisfactory army; certainly no lord with any sense would have tried this after 1100. What the lords wanted was a force of well-trained warriors who would serve anywhere at any time.

Payments to the Lord: Scutage and Aid. If the lord took money instead of service, the interests of both sides were served. The vassal avoided duties which were always inconvenient and often onerous, and the lord acquired funds with which he could hire seasoned soldiers for long campaigns. The most obvious way of raising money was to excuse vassals from service in return for a fixed sum. This was called scutage (shield-money) in England, army aid in France. (*See Reading No. 35.*) If the lord for some reason wanted the services of a particular vassal (usually one of more standing than a simple knight), the vassal might have to pay more than the standard rate in order to be excused. Since the feudal bond was a personal one, in theory the lord could always demand service, whatever amount of money the vassal tendered. In practice, all lesser vassals, and most of the greater ones, could buy themselves off.

It is also in the twelfth century that we first begin to hear of feudal aids—sums paid to the lord by his vassals at times when he had unusual expenses. The most common occasions were the ransoming of the lord from his enemies, knighting of the lord's eldest son (when a great feast would be held and many other young men would be knighted and given horses and armor), and marriage of the lord's eldest daughter (an occasion which even today can be expensive). (*See Reading No. 35.*) In some parts of France an aid was also due when the lord went on a Crusade; in others, when he bought new lands and

[1] The easiest way for this to happen was for a vassal to die and leave only female heirs. The rules of primogeniture did not apply to women. Therefore if a vassal left four daughters, his fief would be equally divided among all four. If he owed 40 days service, each daughter (or her husband) would owe ten.

rights of lordship. At the other extreme, there were areas, such as Germany, where there were none of these customary aids.

Powerful and ambitious lords naturally wanted to take aids more often than two or three times in a reign. They began to ask their vassals (and often their towns and monasteries) for "gracious" aids, usually to meet the expenses of a war. Theoretically, the vassals could always refuse such requests. In practice, they usually felt bound to give their lord something, though it might be less than he had asked. And flat refusals did occur. For example, Henry III of England was unable to persuade his barons to grant any general aid between 1237 and 1269, although he made several requests. Henry's attempts to reconquer lands which John had lost in France, and his support of papal attacks on Sicily, seemed unwise to his vassals, and they therefore refused him financial support. Henry's successor, Edward I (1272-1307), had an entirely different reputation. He was successful, both in diplomacy and in war, and as a result was never refused a general aid.

England is the best example of a country in which aids granted by vassals became so frequent and so essential to government finance that they gradually turned into general taxation. The lords gained nothing by collecting money from their men and turning it over to the king; it saved them time and trouble if royal agents collected the money directly. When this happened, the aid had in effect become a tax on the whole population. But the English barons never yielded on the principle that there must be general consent to aids and to the taxes which developed from them. (*See Reading No. 55.*) Since other men, especially knights and leading burgesses, contributed to the aids and often helped to collect them, the barons gradually came to feel that the consent of these groups was also desirable. This need to obtain formal consent to the granting of an aid was one of the reasons for the development of Parliament as a place and occasion where consent could be given. Similar assemblies developed in other European countries, though often at the provincial rather than the national level.

Relief and Wardship. Aids at first were very infrequent; the lords had to find other ways of making money out of the feudal relationship. Since the fief was at first only a temporary grant, it is likely that heirs, from a very early time, paid the lord something for the right to receive their predecessor's holding. This payment, called "relief," seems to have been moderate at first, but it became excessive in many places, particularly England, in the twelfth century. Again, since a child could not perform feudal service, lords had always entrusted fiefs held by minors to other men who would do the service until the child came of age. This right of wardship had not been an important source of income in the early feudal period. In fact, the lord had often allowed relatives of the minor heir to hold the fief for the benefit of their young relatives. In the twelfth century, in England and parts of France, the lord himself took over the fief, or rented it to a court favorite, thus securing most of the revenues and leaving only a subsistence income for the heir. Finally, since the lord did not wish his vassals to marry his enemies, he could veto the marriage of minor heirs, or of women of any age who become heiresses of fiefs through the death of relatives. From vetoing marriages it was an easy step to selling privileges to marry and, as a final refinement, selling permission to a young lady to reject the suitor whom the king had selected to be her husband. (*See Readings Nos. 36 and 37.*)

The most extreme examples of making large sums of money out of the feudal incidents of relief, wardship, and marriage came from England and northwest France. Elsewhere the rules were more favorable to the vassal. In Germany, and in parts of southern France there was no relief. In the same regions, minor heirs remained in the custody of their relatives, and the lord could not profit from wardship.

Multiple Homages. Nevertheless, while the economic aspect of the feudal relationship was most stressed in England and parts of France, it was important enough everywhere to erode the bond of personal service and personal loyalty. This is seen most clearly in the growth of multiple homages. Originally, a vassal could have only one lord, because the personal relationship was the essential element in the engagement. The soldier needed a commander, and the commander needed soldiers. But when the economic relationship (the fief) became the heart of the agreement, when the lord wanted money and the vassal wanted land, then there was no reason why a vassal could not do homage to many lords. It was natural for a vassal to seek to acquire as many fiefs as possible, and service for each fief could be performed through payments to the appropriate lord. Some effort was made to preserve the principle of personal service by specifying that the vassal's first duty was to his original lord or to the lord from whom he held his principal fief. Homage to this lord was called liege homage, and took precedence over all other engagements. The concept, however, was soon debased. A vassal would do liege homage to his original lord; liege homage to a second lord promising service against all men but the first; liege homage to a third lord, reserving the obligation owed to the first two; and so on. A vassal who had many lords often tried to be neutral when his superiors fought each other or, if he could not be neutral, to join the winning side, even if this meant breaking the rules of liege homage. (*See Reading No. 39.*)

A peculiar example of multiple homage, which appeared soon after 1100, was the money-fief. Here the lord promised the vassal an annual payment from his treasury, in return for a certain amount of service. The vassal obviously already possessed a landed fief and a liege lord, or he would have had no resources with which to render the promised service. Yet the lord who gave the money-fief often succeeded in gaining more service from the vassal than the lord who had given the land. And at the least, the grant of a money-fief usually made the recipient neutral in a war between the two lords. The most famous, and perhaps the oldest example of a money-fief, was the one given to the count of Flanders by the king of England in 1103. (*See Reading No. 38.*) The count held Flanders of the king of France, but during much of the twelfth century he gave diplomatic, and at times military aid to the king of England, and considerably less assistance to the king of France. It is true that the count had other reasons to seek English friendship: his industrial towns needed English wool, and he himself was worried by the growing power of the French king. But similar arrangements were made for much less important men, men who had neither the commercial nor the political problems of the count of Flanders. In these cases, too, the money-fief proved about as effective as the older landed fief in securing the services, or at least the good will, of the recipient.

The Fief as Property. Another sign of the decay of personal service was the growing tendency to treat the fief as a piece of property, instead of a temporary device for supplying a soldier with his equipment and rations. All through the twelfth century, hereditary rights to fiefs were strengthened. Children, women, remote heirs were allowed to inherit fiefs. One of the ways in which great lords strengthened their relations with rear-vassals was by protecting the rights of such heirs against greedy barons or neighbors. At the same time, buying and selling of fiefs became common. (*See Readings No. 49 and 51.*) The lords usually demanded a fee for confirming such transactions, but after some initial resistance, they showed no repugnance to the idea that a fief could be sold. Since they no longer expected much personal service, it mattered little to them who held the fief. They received the same payments whether the holder were a man or a woman, an old friend, or a stranger from the next county.

— 11 —

THE RISE OF THE KNIGHTS AND CHIVALRY

The Feudal Social Group. While the emphasis on the economic relationship weakened feudalism as a military institution, it had less influence on feudalism as a form of political and social organization. Lords and vassals were still the group which had a monopoly of political power and of the perquisites of political power. They had all the rights of government, of justice, and of administration, and all these rights were sources of profit. With the building of feudal systems and the transformation of lesser vassals from professional fighters into small landlords, the feudal group became more united and more homogeneous than it had ever been before. The sharp line between the governing group of counts and their deputies, and the fighting group of knights had been erased. By the end of the twelfth century almost every member of the feudal group, great lords and petty knights, had some share of political power and some feeling of belonging to the same social group. (*See Reading No. 42.*) As we have seen, there had been a time when many knights would not have been considered noble; after 1200, the mere fact of being a knight was considered a sign of nobility. The change was slowest in Germany, where there had been the largest number of knights of obviously servile origin. The change was most peculiar in England, where the knights became socially, but not legally, members of the noble class. A rich knight could easily marry the daughter of an earl, but he was still legally a commoner, while the earl was a nobleman. But even with these hesitations and restrictions, Western Europe had come a long way from the social conditions of the early feudal period. A new aristocracy of lords and gentlemen had been created—an aristocracy which held a dominant place in European life well into the nineteenth century.

One should also note that while vassals disliked the idea of unpaid military service, many of them thoroughly enjoyed fighting when there was some profit in it. A king who hired mercenaries usually hired a good many knights, either his own or those of some other lord. Some of the army, especially bowmen and other foot soldiers, would be simple peasants, but a large part of the cavalry and most of the officers would be members of knightly or baronial families. Not all men of these families wanted to fight, but those who did could easily find employment somewhere. Many of them had to hire themselves out as soldiers because of economic necessity. The younger son of a poor knight or even of a minor baron would have little enough to live on if he were not paid by some great lord. Thus the new aristocracy of lords and gentlemen became the reservoir from which the key men in armies were recruited, and this practice also continued almost to our own day.

Chivalry. The rise in social position and the fact that the knights were now an elite group, both in government and in armies, were two of the factors which produced the concept of chivalry. The increased prosperity of the twelfth century and the growth of new cultural interests also had their effect. Prolonged meetings of knights and lesser barons at the courts of great lords were now possible, and these men could not spend all their time hunting or fighting. There was need for some form of indoor amusement—singing, dancing, story-telling—and some need to impress the ladies with one's social accomplishments. Finally, the twelfth century was the great century of the Crusades, and out of this experience came the picture of the knight as the soldier of God, the protector of the innocent, and the avenger of evil. At this time the Church began to take part in the ceremony by which a man became a knight—a ceremony which had scarcely existed in earlier centuries. (*See Reading No. 43.*) Thus, the idea gradually became established that to receive knighthood was a certificate of social acceptability. The ideal knight was pictured as a courteous and pleasant companion, a man who knew something of music and poetry (*see Reading No. 44*), a man whose real liege lord was God, and whose enemies were the enemies of the faith. We know something of the knights of this period: not many of them lived up to this ideal, though a few, like the great William Marshal of England, came close. (*See Reading No. 41.*) But the fact that the ideal existed is important. It is part of the process by which knights became accepted as members of the nobility. It is the beginning of the formulation of the idea of the gentleman. By the thirteenth century, even kings felt that some precious quality was added when they received knighthood; in the ninth century they most assuredly would not have felt the need for such a ceremony.

I have already suggested that the great lords profited more from the creation of feudal systems than did lords at the intermediate level. The same thing was true of the economic and social changes which we have just described. The intermediate lords, barons, castellans, and the like, could collect money from petty vassals, but they had to pay almost equally large sums in their turn to their superiors. In England, for example, when a scutage was collected, the king took great pains to be sure that he received as much from his barons as the barons received from their knights. It was only the very greatest lords-kings, and some dukes and counts, who received money from many vassals and gave money to no one. Moreover, even if a castellan, through custom, carelessness, or special favor, was allowed to keep most of the money he received from his vassals, he still did not greatly improve his position. One could not hire many mercenaries or buy many allies with the scutages paid by thirty or forty knights. In the new dimensions of twelfth-century warfare it took thousands of pounds to conduct a campaign, and the average castellan had an income counted in hundreds of pounds. In fact, the castellan was more likely to hire himself out as a mercenary leader than to try to raise an independent mercenary force of his own.

The rise in status of the knights had similar effects. The knight was certainly not the equal of a count or an earl, even if he was on the fringe of the same social class, but a knight might easily think himself the equal of some of the lesser barons or castellans. In England, where it was legally important to draw the line between knight and baron, it is evident that there was some difficulty in doing so—a man listed as a baron in one year will be called a knight the next, and vice-versa. Moreover, ambitious knights sought the courts of the great lords, not dismal castles of the rulers of a few peasant villages. There they learned the arts of chivalry, and even more important, some of the new techniques of government. Lords of the intermediate group, if they wished to hold their own with the abler knights, found it advisable to play the same game; they went to the great courts and sought the favor of great men.

— 12 —

THE BEGINNINGS OF BUREAUCRACY

Problems of Administration. These tendencies aided the next step in the development of feudalism—the creation of a rudimentary bureaucracy. As feudal systems grew, as the cash income of certain lords increased, as the prestige of the great courts grew, it became possible to think of exerting real power over an area larger than a few castellanies. The creation of a feudal system with its theory of delegated rights gave the superior lord excuses for extending his power, and increased revenues gave him the military power necessary to enforce his claims. But once the lesser lord had been humbled or dispossessed, what was to be done with his holdings? To give them out again as a fief added little to the victor's strength and almost guaranteed another controversy at some time in the future. To farm them out—that is, to give them to a man in return for a fixed yearly revenue —was almost as bad. If the holder of the farm were vigorous and able, he would soon make the farm an hereditary fief. If, to avoid this danger, the lord picked a man of low origin (and many did), then the holder of the farm might be too weak to protect the lord's rights. And, weak or strong, the holder of the farm almost invariably cheated his lord and oppressed his subjects. It was a great temptation to multiply fines in petty courts of justice, to increase tolls, to demand new "presents" from the peasants, since everything collected over the fixed yearly sum was kept by the farmer.

Obviously, the best thing to do with newly acquired territories was to administer them directly from the lord's court. Small fiefs and small farms, not big enough to become independent, could be allowed to survive. But the lord needed agents to make his presence felt throughout his new domains, to hear important cases and to collect important revenues.

The difficulty was to find such men. In the eleventh century even so great a lord as Duke William of Normandy had no administrative staff. He had a few clerks, but so few that he had to use the aid of monastic scribes when he wanted charters drafted. He had a few knights and barons who spent a good deal of time with him as advisers, and who occasionally acted for him in various parts of the duchy. He had his viscounts, local representatives who were striving, some of them successfully, to become hereditary officials. He had no adequate system of record-keeping, no assurance that he was getting all the revenue due him, no way of trying all the cases which should have gone to his court, no way of enforcing his orders uniformly throughout his duchy. And at that he was better off than most of his contemporaries because he had held his duchy together and was still obeyed by most of his barons.

Eleventh-century feudal government had been unbelievably simple; the lord, with a handful of vassals and a clerk or two, did the few things which had to be done in a very informal way. The clerks, trained for the most part in monastic schools, had had little preparation for administrative work. They had none of the skill in the use of precise legal language or the love of preserving precedents and records which marked their thirteenth-century successors. The vassals were even more completely amateurs in the art of government. No one had any illusions about the competence of these early feudal courts. In any serious dispute over land or feudal rights, any sensible man would urge the parties to accept arbitration rather than ask for a court judgment. Courts themselves frequently gave the same advice. Arbitration agreements not only had a better chance of being observed than court orders, they also relieved members of the court from the ainful task of deciding issues which they did not really nderstand.

Professional Administrators: The Clerks. These simle methods would not do for the twelfth century. As the se of mercenaries increased, as the practice of buying llies with money-fiefs grew, as fortifications became more laborate and more expensive, exact accounting and careul financial management became more necessary. As the ourts of justice of the greater lords became more active nd more powerful, some legal principles had to be estabshed. In short, there was now a need for professional, r at least semi-professional administrators and judges. 'his need was filled in two ways. The growing interest ı learning which culminated in the establishment of the rst universities meant that during the twelfth century ıere was a steady increase in the number of educated ıen. These men were often lawyers, but whether they 'ere students of law, or mere masters of arts, they were rilled in the skills of precise definition and logical thinkıg, which was just what was needed to establish the preedents and routines of orderly administration. Many of ıem served the church, either before or concurrently with ıeir service of lay rulers, and church administration was ır ahead of that of any lay government. These educated nd experienced clerks made it possible for the great lords) profit from their new opportunities. They devised ways) improve the collection and accounting of the lord's :venues; they worked out the procedures and preserved ıe precedents which made the lord's courts more effecve. In England these men were keeping detailed financial :cords (the Pipe Rolls) and writing treatises on English .w before the middle of the twelfth century. (*See Readıgs Nos. 30, 31, 32, 36, and 37.*) By the end of the :ntury such activities were common in most of the feualized area of Europe.

Professional Administrators: The Laymen. The :illed clerk could formulate rules and keep records, but : could not enforce his lord's rights. The indispensable ement of power had to be added by laymen—men who ɔuld act as local judges, administrators, and revenue ɔllectors. It had always been harder to find trustworthy laymen than trustworthy clerks, but the social changes of the twelfth century made the task somewhat easier. Some members of the feudal aristocracy had ceased to consider war their main occupation and were trying to make the most out of their position as landlords. They were not always as successful in this occupation as they could have wished; indeed, many knights and some lesser barons were barely able to live as a gentleman should. Below the class of needy gentlemen was the rising class of the bourgeoisie—a group which had scarcely existed before the late eleventh century, but which now included many able and ambitious men. Many gentlemen, and most of the bourgeoisie, had received at least a rudimentary education from private tutors or elementary schools set up in the towns. The literate layman was no longer a rarity. And in both classes there was a growing desire for more order and security, for more government and better government.

Thus, when the rulers of feudal principalities wanted to recruit laymen as administrators, they had several things in their favor. There were many country gentlemen who had too much spare time and not enough spare money. There were businessmen who were quite eager to gain prestige and profit by serving a great lord. By offering good salaries, or the prospect of gifts of land, lords could find an adequate number of laymen and start building a corps of administrators. Recruitment was at first on a rather casual basis; the lord simply picked men he happened to know for specific jobs he wanted done. Some men proved good at this work, and were used again and again. They gradually became semi-professional administrators who developed traditions and procedures for their offices. Also, like most officials of all periods, they soon found that they needed deputies and assistants. The result was that in the most advanced feudal principalities, the beginnings of a civil service could be seen by the end of the twelfth century. Men started in subordinate posts, learned basic administrative procedures, and then were promoted if they gave satisfaction. Most of these lay administrators came from the ranks of the lesser feudal aristocracy. It was only toward the end of the century that a few businessmen received really important offices

A typical lay administrator was the *bailli,* who began to appear in France about 1180 (*see Reading No. 45*), but who reached the height of his power only after 1200. He was the administrative head of a sizable district; he was responsible for justice, finance, police, and defense. (*See Reading No. 46.*) He was paid a good salary, but was seldom allowed to stay in one district for more than four or five years. He might then be given another district to rule, or be appointed to a position in the central government. His power was temporary, and came only from his office. No *bailli* ever had life tenure, much less an expectation of leaving his position to his son. No *bailli* ever succeeded in using his office to build up a lordship for himself, though some of them became wealthy men. Most *baillis* were knights or lesser barons; a few came from the bourgeoisie. Their subordinates came from the same classes and were subject to the same rules.

In England the circuit judges, who go back at least to the 1120's, played much the same rôle. They traveled about the country in teams of four or five, some laymen and some ecclesiastics. They held court in the counties they visited, and they investigated the work—especially the financial work—of county officials. (*See Reading No. 47.*) As opposed to France, however, these emissaries of the king did not stay long in any one place. Unpaid local notables—chief of whom was the sheriff—did most of the detailed work of local administration. England was small enough, and the king was strong enough, so that there was little danger of usurpation of power. But there was a steady tendency to exclude the great nobles from lay administrative positions. In the early 1100's most sheriffs and most lay circuit judges were men of baronial rank. In the thirteenth century the same positions were filled by country gentlemen—well-to-do knights and squires.

Germany never developed an effective central government in the Middle Ages (*see Reading No. 50*), but the German principalities did eventually acquire groups of lay administrators. In Italy political power in the north gradually passed from the feudal nobility to the municipal governments. In the south, the kingdom of Sicily (which included not only the island, but the southern third of the peninsula) had a highly centralized government in the twelfth century, a government run by a bureaucracy in which feudal barons had almost no power.

Relations Between Feudal Lords and Professional Administrators. Thus, everywhere in Europe it was becoming possible, at least in theory, to control and administer wide territories without the aid of the feudal aristocracy. Few rulers went this far, but at least they could supplement the services and supervise the activities of feudal lords through a corps of administrators who were entirely dependent on the central authority. Since the corps of administrators was drawn very largely from families of acceptable social standing, and since a considerable number of feudal lords were not very anxious to spend long hours on government work, it was not difficult to work out a rough division of authority. Lords were left enough power to control the peasants on their estates, but all important or difficult governmental problems were handled by professional or semi-professional administrators.

Once more, this was a development which was more profitable to kings and the greater lords than to petty counts and barons. The great men had more to offer and a larger population to draw from; they had no trouble in recruiting administrators. The ruler of a small county controlled few ecclesiastical benefices; he had little land to give away, and not much money with which to pay salaries. He often found it difficult to build even a rudimentary administrative service. If he had a powerful neighbor, these weaknesses soon made it impossible for him to keep his independence. Thus the king of France found it easy to absorb a number of the small principalities on his eastern frontier. (*See Reading No. 51.*) On a smaller scale, the count of Savoy played the same game in the area between France and Italy. The small, independent feudal state survived only in places like the Rhineland and the Netherlands which were remote from any of the great rulers.

— 13 —

THE AFTERMATH OF FEUDALISM

Slow Growth of the Modern State. Some scholars argue that feudalism, in its strict sense, came to an end soon after 1200, as a result of the charges which have just been described. The vassal-lord relationship had ceased to be important, either as a means of raising an army or as a way of getting the work of government done. The tendency toward fragmentation of political power had been reversed. Large political units were being built in many parts of Europe, and even in the smaller principalities there was a growing concentration of power in the hands of the ruler. Public officials, appointed by the king or the prince, were supplanting men who held political power as a private possession. In short, the sovereign state was emerging, and feudalism was becoming a matter of empty formalities.

Much of this is true, but feudalism, like any political institution which has had any vitality, was a long time a-dying. Certainly some thirteenth-century thinkers had the concept of the sovereign state, but it took at least two centuries for this concept to be fully realized. Meanwhile, many of the conditions which had made feudalism possible persisted: poor communications, a largely agricultural population, concentration on local interests, scanty public revenues, a shortage of trained manpower, and a tradition of respect for aristocratic leadership. Change in any of these conditions was slow, and subject to many setbacks. For example, the economic boom of the twelfth and early thirteenth centuries was followed in the fourteenth century by a depression which drove most governments into bankruptcy. This led, especially in France, to the sale of public offices as a way of raising money. Public offices, at first sold only for life, soon became heritable, and thus the sale of offices led to the creation of a new hereditary officeholding class. War and plague deprived rulers of some of their ablest administrators. It was not easy to create the structure of the modern state, and while it was being built rulers had to use fragments of the older system as stop-gaps and temporary expedients. Remnants of feudal institutions were embedded in the structure of every modern European state, and ideas derived from feudalism persisted into the nineteenth century.

Everywhere in Europe, the landed aristocracy retained privileges and special powers throughout the later Middle Ages and early modern period. This was not just a matter of traditions which had been sanctified by law, nor was it due to the fact that young princes who received an aristocratic education naturally preferred to associate with aristocrats with a similar education when they came to the throne. Much more important was the fact that no ruler could yet envisage building the kind of civilian and military bureaucracy which would do all the work of the state. This was partly due to lack of money. Why pay for local government when a great deal of it would be done for nothing by local landlords? It was also due to lack of imagination. When things went well, the old methods were good enough; in time of stress it was easier to appoint temporary officials and commissions than to create permanent new administrative organizations. There was always the hope that the emergency, even so common an emergency as war, would not recur, and that after the crisis the government could return to its old pattern. Shortages of money and lack of imagination explain why it took so long to establish standing armies, and even longer to create permanent ministries of war and of the navy. But if governments would not pay for some jobs, and refused to put others on a permanent basis, then they had to rely on the landed aristocracy. These were the only people who could afford to give unpaid or intermittently paid service as administrators, or as officers in the army. At the least, by rendering these services they could justify their privileged position and might add something to their ordinary income. At the best, there was always the gamble that service to the king or success in war might lead to royal favor and hence to great wealth and prominence. Few professional civil servants, few members of the bourgeoisie wanted to take such a gamble.

Aristocratic Control of Local Government. Even in France, which had the largest and most complex bureaucracy in Europe, a great deal of the work of local government was left to the aristocracy. The courts of the seigneur settled the quarrels of a large part of the peasantry. Granted that these courts were supervised by royal officials, it is still true that the lord or his agent had a good deal of freedom in dealing with the peasants. (*See Readings Nos. 53 and 54.*) Other bureaucratic states on the Continent followed much the same pattern. In England, which had a very small bureaucracy, the control of the landowners over local government was even greater. In the thirteenth century, sheriffs, collectors of taxes, and special commissioners were all local landholders, and all unpaid. During the fourteenth century the Justices of the Peace gradually became the chief agents of local government. These men were drawn almost entirely from the ranks of the gentry (landlords) and their relatives and allies, the lawyers, and they ruled England down to the time of the Industrial Revolution.

Aristocrats and the Army. The unpaid jobs were largely in local government; the intermittent ones in military affairs. When thirteenth- or fourteenth-century rulers wanted to raise an army, they usually commissioned men of noble rank to do the work of recruiting for them. Each captain raised his own company and was paid according to its size. (*See Reading No. 56.*) When the war was over, the company was supposed to be disbanded, but if it had proved to be a good fighting unit, the captain often tried to hold it together. It was *his* company, not that of the man who had hired him, and he could always look for another employer. The Englishman, Sir John Hawkwood, took his company to fight in the wars among the city-states of Italy. He must have been fairly honest, since the grateful Florentines placed his portrait in their cathedral. Other less scrupulous captains simply plundered weakly defended areas. Usually it was the peasants and inhabitants of small towns who suffered most from these brigands, but one leader extorted money from the pope by threatening to attack the papal residence at Avignon.

This combination of influence in local affairs and control over armed forces has led some writers to speak of the "bastard feudalism" or the "new feudalism" of the fourteenth century. It is true that in many areas there were men with bands of armed retainers who dominated local government, and that this was the sort of situation which had produced feudalism in the ninth century. It is also true that central governments for a time seemed to be unable to cope with these armed bands, that civil war became endemic in England, France, and Germany, and that large areas of these countries were controlled or devastated by rival warlords. And yet if we can forget the human suffering involved, the "new feudalism" was not very dangerous. It was, in the first place, too dependent on central governments to wish to overthrow them. The captain and his men wanted to be paid in cash (not land), and the only regular source of cash was a reasonably strong government. In the second place, fourteenth- and fifteenth-century central governments, unlike those of the ninth and tenth centuries, were actually growing stronger during the period of crisis. In spite of all difficulties, they were improving their administrative and financial techniques and increasing the number of professional civil servants. They made a deliberate and, in the end, successful effort to keep the captains of armed bands from becoming independent. The passage of laws against livery and maintenance (illegal armed bands) in England and the creation of a royal standing army in France are examples of such acts. Finally, the power of the warlords was ephemeral. No aristocratic military chief succeeded in gaining the permanent loyalty of a province, or hereditary leadership for his family. The Percies in England, the Armagnacs in France quickly lost their special position. Even the Duke of Burgundy, who was much more than a local warlord, failed in his effort to establish a new Middle Kingdom. In short, the "new feudalism" did not splinter old kingdoms as the original feudalism had done.

Continuing Aristocratic Influence in Politics and Education. There were, however, three important results of the continuing power of the aristocracy in the later Middle Ages. In the first place, they acquired a near monopoly of certain civil and military offices. In every county the officer corps was dominated by aristocrats; it was rare for a plebeian to gain a position of command. In every country the highest positions in the Church were reserved for men of noble blood. In every country the Council, the center of executive power in the later Middle Ages, was filled with great lords, or at least with well-to-do country gentlemen. There were ways, of course, of evading the monopoly. The office reserved for an aristocrat could be turned into a purely ceremonial position, while the real work was done by a bourgeois deputy; or able bourgeois officials could be ennobled so that they could hold the highest posts. But the fact that these expedients were necessary shows how strong the aristocratic claims were. It took two centuries of absolutism and one century of revolution to weaken their monopoly; in fact, both absolutism and revolution were reactions to the continuing power and prestige of the aristocracy.

In the second place, the aristocracy continued to develop a pattern of training for its youth, a pattern which began with chivalry, but which in the end came to include also the new learning of the Renaissance. This created standards which dominated European—and even American—education for centuries. Physical training, especially in riding and fencing, continued to be important, but physical training was no longer enough. A certain degree of literacy was necessary to hold positions in local government or the army; even some legal knowledge was thought desirable in England and other regions ruled by customary law. A good many English gentlemen spent a year or two at the Inns of Court (the English law-schools); a good many French gentlemen read treatises on the laws of their particular province. More than this, a young aristocrat who wanted social success had to know something about literature and music. The books he read (or heard read) were largely in the vernacular, but a considerable amount of classical literature was translated, paraphrased, or echoed in writings in the vernacular. And the number of gentlemen who could read Latin with some ease increased during the thirteenth and fourteenth centuries. Life at the court of a king or a great noble was itself an education—in manners and in taste, in politics and in administration. In short, by the fifteenth century the ideal aristocrat had been trained in the physical skills needed for combat, the social skills needed for court life, and the intellectual skills needed for leadership. The ideal of a liberal education was beginning to emerge, with its rejection of professional training and its emphasis on the humanities.

The Aristocracy and Representative Assemblies. Finally, as has already been suggested, the position and power of the aristocracy was a principal cause of the growth of representative assemblies in Europe in the thirteenth and fourteenth centuries. States emerging from the feudal experience found it essential to secure the consent of the propertied classes to many acts of government. There was no place for taxation in feudalism, only for aids granted by vassals to their lord. There was great sensitivity about changing the law, since the law protected feudal rights; therefore a sensible ruler consulted some or most of his vassals before changing the law. And even after all the centralization of the thirteenth century, it was still difficult for any government to enforce its orders anywhere without the cooperation of local notables—that is, outside the cities, the landed aristocracy. Publicity and propaganda as well as military power were necessary to get this cooperation.

At the same time, the court of a feudal lord, where consent could be given and cooperation secured, could very easily be turned into a representative assembly. It was almost impossible, in a principality of any size, for all the prelates and vassals to come to any one meeting. By the thirteenth century, it was recognized that those absent were bound by the acts of those present or, in other words, that those present represented their class. (*See Reading No. 58.*) It was equally impossible for an entire community to appear in court, and yet there were cases where a town, a county, or a religious establishment had to defend its rights. It could only do so by sending agents or attorneys—that is, representatives. All that was needed to make a court into a representative assembly was to formalize this process: to summon a few great

nen as individuals, and to order the lesser aristocracy
ınd the privileged towns to send representatives. This
step was taken almost everywhere in Europe in the thir-
eenth and fourteenth centuries, beginning in Italy, Spain,
ınd southern France, then spreading to England, north-
rn France, and the Germanic countries.

The function, powers, and organization of these assemblies varied greatly from country to country. They could
be used to give consent to taxation, to approve new laws,
ınd to hear explanation of policy. They could be merely
ıdvisory and consultative bodies, or they could have full
power to deny taxation and block legislation. They could
be organized on a national or on a provincial basis. Their
nternal structure could encourage or hinder cooperation
ımong classes. But wherever they existed, and as long as
they met frequently, they were a constant reminder of one
of the basic characteristics of feudalism—the division of
political power among the privileged classes, and the re-
ulting limitations on the power of the ruler.

Obviously, the assembly which did the most work, had
the most power, and best secured the cooperation of the
privileged classes was the assembly which had the greatest
hance for survival. Various historical accidents put the
English Parliament in this position. It met frequently; it
poke for the whole country; it acted on all important
questions of taxation and legislation. In an age of coups
nd revolutions its approval was sought to legitimatize
overnments of dubious legality. For our purposes, how-
ver, the most important characteristic of the English
Parliament was that each of its two houses was controlled
y the aristocracy. The House of Lords was composed
f barons and prelates; the House of Commons was
ominated by country gentlemen. These were largely rela-
ives, friends, and retainers of the barons—that is, the
escendants of the old class of lesser vassals. The towns-
nen usually followed the lead of the gentry; in fact, as
me went on most of the towns formed the habit of elect-
ng country gentlemen as their representatives.

This domination by the aristocracy stiffened the Eng-
sh Parliament. In times of crisis it could speak with one
oice for all the powerful and wealthy men of England;
could defy and, in the end, break the power of kings.

The weakness of many other assemblies was that the aristocracy took no interest in them and pursued its interests through intrigues with courtiers and officials. This was never the case in England during the crucial period of transition from medieval to early modern monarchy. And it is because the English aristocracy dominated both Parliament and English local government that so many elements of feudal custom have persisted in the law and institutions of the English-speaking world.

* * *

It is a far cry from the bodyguards of Germanic chieftains and the counts of Charlemagne to the country gentlemen of eighteenth-century England or the courtiers of Louis XV. Yet one thing had persisted during all these centuries—the feeling that a certain class was born to fight, to command, and to govern, and that it was impolitic, immoral, and unjust for any king to disregard these claims. This feeling caused the aristocratic reaction of the eighteenth century which in its turn led to the great revolutions, which, above everything else, were attacks on special privileges. A drive for political power by the aristocracy led to the rise of feudalism; an attack on the political power of the aristocracy wiped out the last remnants of the feudal tradition.

Part II
READINGS

— Reading No. 1 —

DESCRIPTION OF THE GERMAN *COMITATUS* BY TACITUS, c. 98 A.D.[1]

The chief works of the great Roman historian Tacitus dealt with the emperors of the first century A.D. These rulers had many conflicts with the Germans, which may be why Tacitus also wrote a short article on Germany. He probably never visited the country, but got his information from traders and envoys. He is not always accurate, but this early description of the German war-band (comitatus) *corresponds well with later accounts. Notice that the relationship between leader and retainer is a highly honorable one, and that retainers may be men of high birth.*

It is not customary for anyone to assume arms until the tribe has recognized that he is competent to use them. Then in a full assembly one of the chiefs or the father or relatives of the youth give him the shield and spear. . . . Distinguished birth, or the great merit of their fathers, can cause chiefs to look favorably on mere adolescents. These [boys] join with others who are stronger and more experienced, and they are not ashamed to be looked on as followers [*comites*]. Among the war-band [*comitatus*] there are different ranks, assigned by the judgment of the leader. There is also great competition among the follow-

[1] From Tacitus, *Germania*, ch. 13.

ers to rank first in the eyes of the chief, and among the chiefs as to who shall have the largest and fiercest group of fighters. Both power and prestige came from always being surrounded by a large band of carefully chosen young men; they are an honor in peace and a protection in war. It brings fame and glory to a leader not only in his own folk, but among neighboring peoples, if his war-band is superior in numbers and courage.

When they go to war it is a disgrace for the chief to be outdone in deeds of valor, and for the followers not to equal the courage of their chief. Moreover, for a follower to survive his chief and come unharmed out of a battle is life-long infamy and shame. . . . The chief fights for victory, the men for their chief.

If the folk to which they belong sinks into the lethargy of a long peace, many of the noble young men seek other peoples who are making war. . . . It is easier to gain a great reputation in the midst of perils, and a large following cannot be preserved except through violence and war. They depend on their chief for their war-horse, and their weapons; they consider their [minimum] pay to be the feasts [which he provides], but the real wealth [which attracts them] comes from war and plunder.

— Reading No. 2 —

PRIVATE ARMIES IN THE LATE ROMAN EMPIRE, FIFTH CENTURY[1]

These extracts from laws of the emperors Theodosius II (408-450), Valentinian III (422-455), and Leo I (457-474) show that minor officials and private persons, as well as generals, had their own bands of armed men. They also show that these private soldiers of the Late Empire were of low social position—slaves, barbarians, and Isaurians (a rather primitive people of Asia Minor).

Law of Theodosius II, 444 A.D.

Valerianus, a curial [member of a town council] of Emesa, . . . assumed for himself unjustly and surreptitiously the insignia of a high office. . . . [then] accompanied by a great horde of barbarians, he rushed into the private council chamber of the governor of the province and . . . seated himself on the right of the man to whom we have committed the laws. . . . When he had put to flight all the office staff of the governor, he left everything devastated and deserted. . . . He placed a garrison of slaves in opposition to the tax collectors, contrary to

[1] The first two selections are from the *Theodosian Code* (Nov. Th. 15, 2; Nov. Val. 13), vol. II, pp. 36, 97 of the Mommsen-Meyer edition. The third selection is from Justinian's Code, ix, 12, 10.

public discipline, and thereby our treasury suffered a great loss through his madness.

Law of Valentinian III, 445 A.D.

It shall also be the responsibility of the duke of the province that no one shall be allowed to have armed men, thus creating an opportunity of harassing others, except perhaps those persons who at their own risk with praiseworthy animosity against the enemy have promised their own bands of soldiers and their own forces for the common welfare. . . . Such men shall have for themselves whatever booty of the enemy they have acquired. . . .

Law of Leo I, 468 A.D.

We forbid everyone in town or country to have private soldiers [*bucellarii*] or Isaurians or armed slaves. If anyone . . . shall attempt to have armed slaves or private soldiers or Isaurians on his property or near him, after a fine of 100 pounds of gold, we order a most severe punishment for them.

— Reading No. 3 —

A GENERAL FORMULA OF COMMENDATION, SEVENTH CENTURY[1]

This document shows how free men could become dependents of the great lords. In this formula the service to be rendered was not defined, and the retainer may not have been used as a soldier. But men who did specialize in military service made the same kind of promises and did not necessarily receive anything more than food and clothing from their lords.

✓ ✓ ✓

To the magnificent lord *so-and-so,* I *so-and-so.* Since everyone well knows how little I have with which to feed and clothe myself, I have therefore appealed to your charity, and you have been willing to allow me to hand myself over or commend myself to your protection. This I have done on these conditions: You are to aid and support me with food and clothing, insofar as I shall be able to serve you and deserve well of you. As long as I shall live, I am bound to give you service and obedience consistent with my status as a free man. For the rest of my life I shall have no power to withdraw from your lordship and protection, but all the days of my life I must remain under your power and defense. Therefore it is agreed that if one of us tries to withdraw from these agreements, he shall pay *so many* shillings to the other party, and the contract shall remain in force.

[1] From *M. G. H., Formulae Merowingici et Karolini aevi,* ed. K. Zeumer (Hannover, 1886), p. 158.

— Reading No. 4 —

AN EARLY FORM OF VASSALAGE
(First Half of Seventh Century)[1]

The Frankish king, like his predecessors, had a bodyguard, who in the seventh century were called "antrustiones." Here we have an early example of one of these men taking an oath "in the hand," a form which became an essential part of feudal homage. (See Reading No. 8.) *The rising status of the "antrustion" is indicated by the fact that killing him brings a penalty ("wergeld") of 600 shillings, three times that of an ordinary freeman.*

✓ ✓ ✓

It is right that those who promise us unbroken faith should be placed under our protection. And because *so-and-so,* our faithful man [*fidelis,* = vassal in some later texts] has come here in our palace with his weapons, and has sworn, in our hand, loyalty and fidelity, therefore, by this present document, we decree and order that from now on he be considered one of our body of "antrustiones." And if anyone should dare to kill him, let him know that he will be liable to pay a "wergeld" of 600 shillings.

[1] From *M. G. H., Formulae,* ed. K. Zeumer (Hannover, 1886), p. 55.

— Reading No. 5 —

A FORMULA FOR GRANTING A *PRECARIA*, SEVENTH CENTURY[1]

This is one of a number of formulae which were collected in the seventh century to teach scribes how to draw up documents in proper form. The precaria, *a grant of land to a dependent for the term of his life, was one of the most common of these formulae. By granting a* precaria *the owner gained a regular rent (and sometimes services); the dependent gained the protection of the lord and some land to cultivate. The fief given to a military retainer (at first only for the term of his life) is a specialized development of the* precaria. (See Reading No. 6.)

✓ ✓ ✓

To the venerable father in Christ, the lord abbot so-and-so . . . I, in God's name, come to you with a request for a grant of land. And according to my request, you, with the consent of your brother monks, have ordered that your property in a place called *so-and-so,* in the county of *so-and-so* . . . may be given to me through your goodness[2] to enjoy and cultivate. . . . And I promise you that I will give you for this *precaria so many*

[1] From *M. G. H., Formulae,* ed. K. Zeumer (Hannover, 1886), p. 242.

[2] The word translated as "goodness" is "beneficium." A little later grants made on favorable terms to important men were called "beneficia," that is, benefices.

pennies each year . . . , and I shall not lose this property while I live. . . . And after my death it shall revert to your domain with any improvements which I have made, without any claim by my heirs. . . .

— Reading No. 6 —

A FORMULA FOR REGRANTING A GIFT AS A *PRECARIA*, EIGHTH CENTURY[1]

To secure the protection of a church or a great lord, a small landholder sometimes gave his land to a powerful bishop or other potentate and received it back as a precaria.

. . . It is known to all that on this present day I have given my property *in such and such a place* . . . to this house of God. Then you [the bishop or abbot] have agreed that you ought to lend me the use of these lands, while I live. You have done this on these conditions: that I should hold and use the property while I live, and that after my death the officials of the church shall bring the property, with all improvements, under their control, without a formal transfer of title. In return for this *precaria* I promise this house of God that I shall have no power to sell, give or exchange the property nor to take it away from the house of God by any acts or devices. . . .

[1] From *M. G. H., Formulae,* p. 191.

— Reading No. 7 —

AN EARLY FORM OF LAND GRANT TO SOLDIERS, 743 A.D.[1]

The Frankish kingdom was involved in many wars in the eighth century, and the kings were trying to increase the number of heavy-armed cavalrymen. To support these men, they seized church lands and granted them as temporary possessions to their soldiers. This was a special form of the precaria. (See Reading No. 5.) *Though the word fief is not yet used, these grants resemble early fiefs: the holder has no property rights and the land reverts to the lord on his death. The use of church lands for this purpose continued under Charlemagne; probably many fiefs of minor vassals developed from these grants.*

✓ ✓ ✓

Because of the threats of war and the attacks of certain tribes on our borders, we have decided with the consent of our clergy and our Christian people . . . to appropriate temporarily some of the property of the church for the support of our army. The lands are to be held as *precaria* [temporary possessions] and for a fixed rent. Each year one shilling for each peasant household is to be paid to the church or monastery [from which the land was taken]. When the holder dies, the church shall regain possession. If, however, difficult circumstances make it necessary, the ruler may order that the *precaria* be renewed and reassigned.[2]

[1] *M. G. H., Legum,* Section II, ed. A. Boretius (Hannover, 1883), vol. I, p. 9.

[2] The Church actually regained little or none of this land. Charlemagne recognized that return of the land was unlikely, and increased the payments received by the Church as a compensation.

— Reading No: 8 —

HOMAGE OF TASSILO, DUKE OF BAVARIA, 757 A.D.[1]

This is the first example, and one of the few in the Carolingian period, of a great man being explicitly called a vassal. The Franks had not had direct control of Bavaria, and Tassilo had been rebellious. It is possible that the king wished to emphasize Tassilo's defeat and subjection by making him take an oath like that of an ordinary retainer.

King Pippin held his court at Compiègne with the Franks. And there came Tassilo, duke of the Bavarians, who commended himself in vassalage [to the king] by his hands. He swore innumerable oaths, placing his hands on the relics of the saints; he promised fidelity to King Pippin and to his sons, Lord Charles and Lord Carloman, as a vassal should rightly do, with upright mind and firm devotion, such as a vassal should have toward his lords.[2]

[1] *Annales regni Francorum,* ed. F. Kurze (Berlin, 1895), p. 14.

[2] For later descriptions of the vassal's oath, see Readings Nos. 15 and 26.

— Reading No. 9 —

GRANT OF AN IMMUNITY TO A BISHOP, SEVENTH CENTURY[1]

Immunities exempting churches from the authority of royal officials appeared early in the history of the Frankish kingdom. They made the bishop (or abbot) a practically independent local authority. It was only later that laymen received such grants.

. . . Let it be known to you that at the request of that apostolic man, the bishop of *so and so,* and for the salvation of our soul, we have decreed as follows: no public official may enter the estates of this bishop's church, either those which he now holds as gifts . . . or those which may hereafter be granted . . . , for the purpose of trying cases or of collecting fines. But the bishop and his successors shall rule the lands in the name of God with full and complete immunity.

We therefore order that neither you [the count] nor your subordinates, nor your successors, nor any public official is to presume to enter the estates of this church . . . to try cases, collect fines or revenue . . . or to take supplies. All of the fines and other revenues which should come to the royal treasury . . . from the people living on these estates—slave or free, Roman or barbarian—we grant . . . to the church forever. . . .

[1] From *M. G. H., Formulae,* ed. K. Zeumer (Hannover, 1886), p. 43.

— Reading No. 10 —

IMMUNITY GRANTED TO A LAYMAN, 815 A.D.[1]

It had long been customary to grant churches immunity from secular authorities, in order to protect them from greedy counts. Such grants to laymen began later, but had the same effect of weakening the count's power. As soon as royal power declined, an immunity such as this could furnish the nucleus for the creation of an independent lordship.

In the name of our Lord and Savior Jesus Christ, Louis, by the workings of divine providence, Emperor Augustus [Louis the Pious, 814-840 A.D.]: Let it be known to all those who are faithful to Holy Church and ourselves, both present and future, that a certain faithful man of ours, named John, came into our presence and commended himself in our hands. He asked us to confirm the *aprisio* [grant of waste lands[2]] which our father and we gave him, and also whatever since then he and his sons and their men have cleared and occupied, and he showed us the charter which our father gave him. We have ordered to make him another and better charter. We grant

[1] From *Ausgewählte Urkunden,* ed. W. Altmann and E. Bernheim (Berlin, 1895), pp. 262-263.

[2] Much of this part of southern France had been devastated by Moslem raids. Charlemagne and his son were eager to have it restored, and gave extensive privileges to men who would settle there.

our *fidelis* John in the county of Narbonne . . . [various lands] and all the lands which he with his men can clear . . . to be held by him and his sons and their heirs without payment or annoyance.

No count, viscount or any of their subordinates, or any public official shall presume to distrain or judge their men who live on their lands, but John and his sons and their heirs shall judge and distrain them. And whatever they judge lawfully, shall be enforced permanently, and if they go beyond the law, they shall make amends according to law. And that this charter shall have full authority, while he and his sons and their heirs shall remain faithful to us and our sons and their heirs, we have ordered it sealed with our ring.

— Reading No. 11 —

VASSI DOMINICI UNDER CHARLEMAGNE[1]

The "vassi dominici," *direct vassals of the king, were usually men of good family, although not the equals of counts and bishops. Charlemagne relied heavily on their service; at the same time he did not want them to become too independent of the counts, lest local administration break down. In these laws the special status of the* "vassi dominici" *is recognized, but their duties to the count are emphasized. In the end most of the* "vassi dominici" *took root in the counties, became vassals of the counts, and eventually became castellans or other important local lords.*

779 A.D. Thieves taken within an immunity must be brought to the court of the count by their judge; if he fails to do this he shall lose both his benefice [fief] and his office. Likewise if a vassal of ours fails to do this, he shall lose his benefice and his office, and if he has no benefice,[2] he shall pay a fine.

811 A.D. Concerning *vassi dominici* who still serve in the [royal] household, and yet are known to have benefices,[2] we decree thus: those of them who stay with the lord emperor in his household should not keep their vassals who have lands with them. Instead, these [rear]-vassals shall be allowed to serve in the army with the count in whose county they live.

[1] From *Capitularia regum Francorum,* ed. A. Boretius (Hannover, 1883), vol. I, pp. 48, 167, 321.

[2] Note that even a *vassus dominicus* may not have a fief.

823 A.D. (?) Concerning those men who have commended themselves to us, we wish to grant them this privilege above all other free men: wherever they come, either to courts or elsewhere . . . they are to have precedence over everyone, and justice is to be done on their complaints without delay. And their . . . vassals, if they have been with their lords in our service, are not to be impleaded . . . until they return from our service. Then if there is any complaint about them, their lords should be requested to do justice to the plaintiffs, and if the lords [the *vassi dominici*] fail to do this, then legal action may be taken.

— Reading No. 12 —

LETTERS OF EINHARD, 833 and 840 A.D.[1]

Einhard, who had served Charlemagne, had retired from public life before 830, but still had friends at court to whom he wrote letters recommending his friends and followers. These letters show how insecure and unstable the position of a vassal was in the early feudal period.

Einhard to N., eternal salvation.

Frumold, son of count N, . . . worn out by illness rather than by age (for he suffers from a serious and persistent pain in the feet), possesses in Burgundy in the county of Geneva (where his father was once count) a small benefice. He fears that he will lose it unless you are kind enough to aid him, since his illness . . . makes it impossible for him to come to court. Therefore he begs that . . . you will be good enough to ask the emperor [Lothair I] to let him keep this benefice, which the emperor's grandfather [Charlemagne] gave him and the emperor's father [Louis the Pious] allowed him to possess, until he is well enough to come to the imperial presence and commend himself in proper form. Farewell.

[1] From *M. G. H., Epistolae,* ed. K. Hampe (Hannover, 1899), vol. V, *Einharti Epistolae,* nos. 27, 63.

To the reverend and rightly venerable Lord N., priest of the Most High God, Einhard, a sinner.

This vassal named Agantheus, is a relative of mine and was for a while in my service. But because he now desires to live under your lordship . . . I have given him these letters of recommendation[2] . . . so that he may have easier access to your holiness and may settle down near you. I beg you to accept him [as your vassal] and to be kind enough to support him in your service. . . . I wish you good health through the grace of the Lord.

[2] By Frankish law, no one could leave his lord without permission. Einhard's letter was legally necessary, as well as being socially helpful.

— Reading No. 13 —

THE DUTIES OF A NINTH-CENTURY COUNT[1]

These extracts describing the duties of a count come from a capitulary (a series of laws and instructions) issued by Charles the Bald, king of the western part of the Frankish Empire, in 864 A.D. Notice that the count has almost complete power over his country and that some counts are not being very obedient to the king.

1. . . . Counts should consider bishops and other ministers of the Church as their helpers. . . . If any count . . . shall fail to do what we order . . . let the negligence of the count be brought to our attention by the bishops. . . .

4. We order our counts . . . to give respect to the status of our vassals, . . . as they wish to have their own position respected by us. . . .

17. Let the counts . . . see to it that at no place in their counties shall coins be struck secretly or fraudulently. . . .

18. . . . Let each count make a list of all the [public] markets in his county . . . and bring the list to the next meeting of our court, so that we can see what markets are necessary . . . and should be continued . . . and what markets are unnecessary and should be forbidden. . . .

[1] From *M. G. H., Capitularia regum Francorum,* ed. A. Boretius (Hannover, 1897), pp. 313-327.

20. Let the counts . . . and our other *fideles* see that honest measures . . . are made for buying and selling in our towns and villages. . . .

26. The Franks of each county who have horses shall go to the army under their counts. . . .

27. . . . Let the counts diligently inquire how many free men in each county can serve in the army at their own expense. . . .

31. Concerning immigrants from the region which has been devastated by the Northmen, . . . let each count in his county list their names and the names of their lords. . . .

32. Counts whose counties have a common border should not hold their courts on the same day. . . .

35. Let our counts know that we are sending our investigators [*missi*] who are to make a special inquiry about how they are obeying the orders which we are now issuing. . . .

— Reading No. 14 —

THE GREAT COMMANDS UNDER CHARLES THE BALD, 865-868 A.D.[1]

The following extracts come from the part of the Annales Bertiniani *which was written by Hincmar, archbishop of Reims. Hincmar was one of the most powerful and best informed men in the West Frankish kingdom. Notice that it is still helpful to have the favor of the king (Charles the Bald) since he can grant or take away great commands and important counties. But notice also that Charles does not always succeed in making the changes he desires; some men keep their position against his wishes. And Charles' successors were weaker than he.*

✓ ✓ ✓

865 A.D. Charles . . . sent Bernard, son of [count] Bernard and of a daughter of count Rorigo, to Gothia [southwest France] and gave him part of that march [frontier district] to rule.

Charles gave Robert,[2] who was ruler of the march of Anjou [the Breton frontier], the county of Auxerre and the county of Nevers [both far to the east of Anjou] along with his other honors.

When Charles came to Rouy he found that Adelard and his relatives Hugh and Berenger whom he had set to

[1] From *Annales Bertiniani,* ed. G. Waitz (Hannover, 1883), pp. 75, 79, 80, 81, 84, 90.

[2] Robert the Strong, ancestor of the Capetian kings of France.

guard [the Seine valley] against the Northmen, had done nothing useful. So he deprived them of their counties and distributed their offices among several other men.

866 A.D. Charles gave count Robert the abbey of St. Martin[3] . . . and with his advice divided the counties west of the Seine among his supporters. . . .

Normans mixed with Bretons . . . attacked Le Mans. . . . Robert [and other] counts . . . met them at Brissarthe . . . and in the battle Robert was killed. . . . Charles . . . gave Hugh l'Abbé, the son of his uncle Conrad, the county of Touraine, and the county of Anjou with the abbey of St. Martin, . . . and sent him to Neustria[4] in place of Robert.

867 A.D. Charles . . . took the county of Bourges from Count Gerard in his absence, and without any accusation of wrong-doing and gave it . . . to Acfrid.

868 A.D. The men of count Gerard made war on Acfrid . . . and set fire to a house in which he had taken refuge. When Acfrid was driven out, they cut off his head and threw his body in the fire. Then Charles attacked . . . the county of Bourges and did more evil . . . than can be told. However, he not only failed to avenge himself on Gerard and his counts, but he could not even drive them out of the county.

[3] Great lords were often made lay abbots of a rich monastery, to enable them to support their soldiers.

[4] The region between the Loire and the Seine.

— Reading No. 15 —

THE CHURCH AND FEUDALISM, 858 A.D.[1]

This is an extract from a long letter written by Hincmar, archbishop of Reims, to Louis, king of Germany, who had temporarily seized the kingdom of his brother, Charles the Bald of France. Hincmar was speaking for most of the north French bishops, who were not very well disposed toward Louis. Thus the opposition of the prelates to becoming involved in feudal obligations is stated more strongly than it might have been on other occasions. Many bishops did do homage, hold fiefs, and give service just as high-ranking laymen did. Yet the Church was never entirely happy with such arrangements, and Hincmar's objections were revived many times in succeeding centuries.

Notice that to Hincmar "benefice" means an office as well as land, and that a benefice is a fief.

⁂

The churches entrusted to us by God are not royal property, nor benefices of such a sort that the king can give them or take them away as he sees fit, because every thing which belongs to the churches is dedicated to God. . . . And we bishops, consecrated to the Lord, are not men of such a sort that, like laymen, we should commend ourselves in vassalage to anyone . . . nor should we in any fashion take a solemn oath [of homage] which

[1] *M. G. H., Capitularia,* ed. A. Boretius and V. Krause (Hannover, 1897), vol. II, p. 439.

scriptural and apostolical and canonical authority forbid. It is abominable that hands anointed with holy oil, hands which through prayer and the sign of the cross can make the body and blood of Christ out of bread and water . . . that such hands should be touched in a secular ceremony of oath-taking. And it is sinful that the tongue of a bishop, which by the grace of God is a key to heaven, should pronounce an oath over holy relics like any common layman. . . .

— Reading No. 16 —

THE CAPITULARY OF QUIERZY, 877 A.D.[1]

This document was issued by Charles the Bald of the West Frankish kingdom, as he was beginning an expedition to Italy. Meant to cover only problems that might arise during his absence, it nevertheless illustrates relations between king and counts in a period of declining royal power. The king still has the right to appoint anyone he wishes as count, but it is clear that the son or close relative of a deceased count will normally be chosen to replace his kinsman.

If a count shall die, whose son is with us, our son [left behind as regent] with other *fideles* [great lords who had taken a special oath to the king] shall choose from among those who were closest to the count a man who will take care of the county . . . until we are notified. If the count has a minor son the latter, with the officials of the county and the bishop of the diocese . . . shall take care of the county until we are notified, [so that we may honor the son . . . with the offices of his father].[2]

If he has no son, let our son with other *fideles* choose someone . . . to rule the county until we can make a decision. And let no one be angered if we then choose

[1] From *M. G. H., Capitularia,* ed. A. Boretius (Hannover, 1897), vol. II, p. 358.

[2] This phrase was added when the document was read to the assembled army.

to give the county to some other man than the one selected to rule it temporarily. Our vassals [notice that they are distinguished from counts] shall be treated the same way. And we expressly order bishops, abbots, counts and our other *fideles* to make every effort to follow the same rules with their men.

If after our death, one of our *fideles* . . . wishes to enter a religious order, and has a son or a relative capable of giving good service to the state, he [the *fidelis*] may hand over his offices to him.

— Reading No. 17 —

COUNTS AND THEIR COURTS IN THE TENTH CENTURY[1]

These two documents from the county of Mâcon illustrate the gradual shift from public to private authority. The count is still holding a public court, and he is assisted by public officials called scabini. *But the count, and his chief assistant, the viscount, have inherited their position from their fathers, and his other assistants are his* fideles *(vassals). These are the great men of the county; about a century later the descendants of some of them will be castellans holding courts of their own* (see Reading No. 18), *and the count's power will be restricted to the district around Mâcon.*

1) Notice of a quit-claim made at Mâcon, Wednesday, February 12, 951, in the presence of the lord count Leotaldus and his vassals [fideles], viscount Waltherius [son of viscount Maiolus], Ratherius, lord Rotbertus, Teodulfus, Gausbertus, and the *scabini*[2] Bererius, Raymbertus and others. In their presence came two men . . . complaining that . . . their vineyard in Chevagny . . .

[1] From *Recueil des chartes de l'abbaye de Cluny,* ed. A. Bernard and A. Bruel (Paris, 1876, 1880), vol. I, no. 799, vol. II, no. 1179.

[2] The *scabini* were created by Charlemagne to assist counts in their judicial work. They were always prominent local landowners. Often the office was hereditary.

was unjustly held by the monks of Cluny. . . . [Later the monks proved their title, and the plaintiffs relinquished their claim.]

2) Notice of a proclamation in public court, in the presence of the lord count Albericus [son of count Leotaldus], viscount Nardoinus, Vuichardus,[3] Roclenus,[3] Teotbertus, and other *scabini* and good men. . . . There came Giroldus and his wife Gotdoltrudis, complaining that Airoardus held their property in Courcy unjustly. . . . Then came Airoardus . . . with his witnesses, and they swore, so help them God and on holy relics, that Airoardus had a better claim to this property than . . . Giraldus and his wife. These are the witnesses: [7 names]. . . . Given under the hand of Otgerius [a scribe] on Wednesday, June 1, in the tenth year of king Lothair [964].

[3] These men are called *fideles* in other acts of the work cited in note 1, vol. II, nos. 1037, 1087, 1198.

— Reading No. 18 —

AGREEMENT BETWEEN THE LORD OF BUISSIÈRE AND THE MONASTERY OF CLUNY, c. 1060[1]

This agreement was made in the court of a local lord, in the presence of his knights. The count has lost all control over this district, and Cluny (the most important monastery in Europe at this time) does not even think of asking him to intervene. This illustrates the process of fragmentation of political power after 1000 A.D. The county has broken up into castellanies, and each castellan has full rights of justice. The document also illustrates the growing tendency for lords to use knights to help them with their administrative and judicial work.

✓ ✓ ✓

This is the agreement between the monks of Cluny and Hugh de Buissière, in the presence of lord Segaldus, concerning the evil customs[2] which he demands in the lands of Cluny and which his father held justly or unjustly . . . over the serfs of Cluny. . . . He gives all this up in the presence of lord Segaldus . . . except those

[1] From *Recueil des chartes de l'abbaye de Cluny,* ed. A. Bernard and A. Bruel, vol. IV (Paris, 1888), p. 374, no. 3262.

[2] "Customs" can mean many kinds of payments, but at this time it usually includes the profits of justice and thus implies the right to hold a court.

customs which the men of Cluny legally and by custom owe him in his own land. . . . [He also confirms a grant by his brother.] The witnesses who were there are [5 monks]. The knights who held the court are these: Constantin de Mailly, Odulric de Cluny, Licelin and his brother Josseran de Salornay.

— Reading No. 19 —

CHARTER OF COUNT BALDWIN OF FLANDERS, 1038[1]

This charter illustrates two points. In the first place, monasteries which needed protection had to cede valuable rights to their protectors (usually called "advocates"). Count Baldwin is trying to keep these rights from becoming an unbearable burden on the abbey. In the second place, this charter shows knights participating in the court of an important lord at a rather early date.

. . . I, Baldwin, by the grace of God count of Flanders . . . acknowledge and testify before all my barons that the abbey of Marchiennes was always free from obligations to an advocate. . . . However, because of the present evil state of the world, it needs an advocate for its defense. That I may be the faithful advocate and defender of the church, the abbot gave me two mills and two ploughlands in the town of Nesle. . . . I, however, have given the mills and the land with the consent of the abbot to Hugh Havet of Aubigny, so that he may be a ready defender of the church in all things. If he fails in this . . . he shall lose the land and advocacy which he holds of me.

And this is what he receives in the abbey's lordship. He shall have one third of all fines in cases where the church has asked his assistance . . . and has gained

[1] From *Polyptyque de l'Abbe Irminon*, ed. B. Guerard (Paris, 1844), vol. II, pp. 356-357.

something by his justice. . . . If he is not called in, he shall have nothing. . . . In time of war, he shall have . . . from each plough-team two shillings, from half a team one, and from each laborer three pennies. . . . He shall not give orders to the men of the abbey . . . nor hold courts of his own, nor take money from peasants. He is not permitted to buy lands of the abbey, . . . or give its serfs in fiefs to his knights, nor to extort anything from them by violence. . . .

The mark of Baldwin, the marquis,[2] who ordered this document to be made. The mark of Adela, the countess. The mark of Eustace, count of Boulogne. The mark of Roger, count of St. Pol. [Three bishops and five abbots subscribe]. The marks of Sanswalonis, Freardus, Walter, Bernier, Ogier, Dominicus, knights. This court was held by four knights of the advocate: Udo, Ursio, Garderus, Maimbodo. Done at Arras in . . . the year of our Lord 1038. . . .

[2] As usual at this time, count and marquis were interchangeable terms.

— Reading No. 20 —

DECISION OF THE COURT OF THE VISCOUNT OF THOUARS, 1055-1093[1]

This document illustrates the extreme fragmentation of rights of government in the eleventh century. The viscount of Thouars, a vassal of the count of Poitou, has extensive rights of justice, but he allows these to be exercised in part of his domain by two of his subordinates, a prévôt[2] *and a* voyer.[3] *But the monks of St. Aubin of Augers also have rights of justice (a partial immunity) in the same area. The viscount and his court have to decide where the dividing-line between the two authorities lies. Notice that the count of Poitou takes no part in the case; the county as a judicial unit has ceased to exist.*

✓ ✓ ✓

For the sake of peace and harmony, . . . we have ordered this letter drawn up about the controversy . . . between the monks of St. Aubin living at Méron, and the

[1] From *Cartulaire de Saint Aubin d'Angers,* ed. B. de Broussillon (Paris, 1903), vol. I, no. 226, pp. 270-272.

[2] The *prévôt* was usually in charge of a small town or village and the surrounding countryside. He collected rents and administered justice to peasants. Often he made his post hereditary.

[3] The *voyer* was the old *vicarius,* a deputy of the viscount. In many places the castellans took over all the powers of the *voyer.* The few *voyers* who survived were very humble officials. This one is clearly subordinate to the *prévôt.*

prévôt and *voyer* of the viscount of Thouars. The controversy was as follows:

A certain serf of the monks . . . in Montreuil waged a judicial duel which he lost, and he paid the fine which losers customarily pay to the agent of the monks at Montreuil. When he heard this the *voyer* of the viscount demanded the same amount [as a fine] from the serf. But Fulchradus, the monk who ruled this priory . . . claimed before the viscount of Thouars and his court that this demand by the *prévôt* and the *voyer* was unjust. . . .

The viscount and his court decided that it was unjust, because the *prévôt* and the *voyer* have justice in the lands of the monks for only four cases: assault which causes shedding of blood, theft, rape, and arson. Assault, moreover, never leads to a fine to the *voyer,* if it occurred between two men of the monks. Therefore the serf went free, by judgment of the viscount and his court . . . because the judicial duel [on which the *voyer* based his claim] did not arise out of any of these four cases. . . .

[Moreover] sometimes it pleased the *prévôt* or the *voyer* . . . to summon serfs of the monks to their court . . . without telling them the charge against them . . . and if they did not come they paid a fine for contempt. The judgment of the viscount and his barons[4] was that this should not be done in this court. If the *prévôt* or *voyer* of the viscount wish to summon a serf, they must notify him of the charge for which he is being summoned.

[4] The chief vassals of each lord were called his barons. Thus the count of Poitou was a baron of the king of France, the viscount of Thouars was a baron of the count of Poitou, and the viscount's barons included some castellans and some well-born knights.

— Reading No. 21 —

A GRANT BY WILLIAM, DUKE OF NORMANDY (Between 1051 and 1066)[1]

This document illustrates three points about eleventh-century feudalism. First, grants to monasteries by great lords no longer include a grant of full immunity from secular power. Second, the word knight (miles) *is quite ambiguous. The knights given along with peasants and a mill are obviously unimportant men; it is even necessary to specify that they are free. The knights who confirm the duke's grant are great men. Third, a ducal court, composed of a small number of especially trusted vassals, is coming into existence.*

To all those responsible for the care of the holy church of God to whom knowledge of these letters shall come . . . we wish it to be known that the duke of the Normans, William son of Robert, for the welfare of his soul and that of his wife and offspring and also to gain from God all the goods of life on this earth, gave to God and St. Florent [of Saumur] to possess freely and for all times what . . . is listed below: Namely, in the county of the Cotentin the estate called Flottemanville with all its appurtenances, that is, the church and twenty acres, and his

[1] From *Recueil des actes des ducs de Normandie,* ed. Marie Fauroux (Caen, 1961), no. 199.

(the duke's) land of three plough-teams[2] . . . and 12 peasants and five free knights and a mill. And to give permanent validity to this charter, he apposed his mark with his hand,[3] his wife and son did likewise and he then asked his knights to ratify it by their hands . . . These things were given to God and St. Florent and the monks free from all secular dues. . . .[4]

The mark of count William.[5] The mark of countess Matilda. The mark of the count's son. The mark of Robert of Mortain.[6] The mark of William Fitz-Osbern.[6] The mark of Roger of Montgomery.[6] The mark of Richard viscount of Avranches.[6] The mark of Albaldus the monk. The mark of Gumbertus the monk.

[2] Land was often roughly measured by the number of teams needed to plough it. It was frequently reckoned that one plowland equaled 120 acres.

[3] In most documents of this period the donor and witnesses simply made a cross (+) beside their names, which were written by a scribe.

[4] No rights of justice are mentioned.

[5] Duke and count were completely equivalent terms, as far as the Norman rulers of this period were concerned.

[6] These are the "knights" who were intimate advisers of the duke and formed his court. They are all men of importance.

— Reading No. 22 —

FULBERT OF CHARTRES ON THE DUTIES OF A VASSAL, 1020[1]

This extract comes from a letter written to the duke of Aquitaine by bishop Fulbert of Chartres, a famous scholar of the eleventh century. Like most documents of this period it stresses the negative obligations of the vassal; he must not harm his lord in any way. It is very vague on positive duties, though it does use the standard formula of "aid and counsel." This limited interpretation of the vassal-lord relationship was especially accurate when great men were involved. If a count were a vassal of another count, the most the latter could expect was that his vassal would not attack him. Actual service would be a matter for special negotiation.

✓ ✓ ✓

He who swears fealty to his lord ought always to have these six things in mind: what is harmless, safe, honorable, useful, easy, possible. Harmless, in that he should not do his lord bodily harm; safe in that he should not betray his secrets or defenses; honorable, in that he should not weaken his rights of justice or other matters that pertain to his honor; useful, in that he should not attack his possessions; easy or possible in that he should not hinder his lord in doing good . . . or make difficulties in what is possible for his lord to do.

[1] From *Recueil des historiens des Gaules et de la France,* ed. L. Delisle (Paris, 1874), vol. X, p. 463.

However, while it is right that the faithful [vassal] should avoid these injuries, not for this alone does he deserve his holding; for it is not enough to abstain from evil, unless good is done also. Therefore, in addition he should faithfully give aid and counsel to his lord in the six things mentioned above, if he wishes to be looked on as deserving of his benefice and trustworthy concerning his oath of fealty.

The lord also ought to treat his faithful vassal in exactly the same way in all these things. And if he does not, he will justly be considered guilty of bad faith. . . .

— Reading No. 23 —

KNIGHT-SERVICE AND SUBINFEUDATION, c. 1050[1]

This charter, granted by Henry I in 1128, confirms arrangements made by William the Conqueror as duke of Normandy in the 1050's. It shows the beginnings of the creation of a feudal system. The amount of service was carefully specified. William also tried to make sure (as he did on other occasions) that rear-vassals (vassals of his vassals) were men of whom he approved. In this case the feudal chain, duke-lord-knight, would remain unbroken.

I confirm to them [the monks of St. Evroul] the gift of the entire village of Cullei . . . which is one knight's fee [a fief which would support one knight] and the gift . . . of another knight's fee . . . called Bocquencé . . . out of which William my father created a barony to serve him and his heirs in war and in other affairs throughout Normandy. The grant was made on these terms: that Richard de Cullei and Baudri son of Nicholas, knights, to whom . . . the abbot Theodoric gave those two knight's fees with the assent of William my father, to hold by hereditary tenure of the abbot—these two men and their heirs shall serve, each one for his own fief with horses and arms and at his own expense, whenever the

[1] From *Norman Institutions,* by C. H. Haskins (Cambridge, 1925), p. 11. Haskins discusses the probable date (1050-1056) on pp. 11-14.

abbot of St. Evroul shall be summoned by me [the king] and themselves by the abbot. . . . If they shall fail to do service, and the abbot can prove that he summoned them, I and my heirs can punish them bodily, or by confiscating their goods. The abbot shall have relief and justice and the other rights which Norman barons have in the fiefs of their knights. . . .

— Reading No. 24 —

THE TRIAL OF THE BISHOP OF DURHAM, 1088[1]

This account was written a generation after the event, probably by the monk Symeon of Durham. While the author could not have a record of the exact words of the participants, he could have known some of the men involved. He certainly had access to the bishop's records, and he seems to have understood clearly the points of law that were raised. This is one of the best descriptions we have of a trial in a feudal court.

Notice especially that: (*a*) *the bishop, like many other prelates, holds a great fief and so can be treated as a vassal;* (*b*) *he forfeits his fief for failure to give service;* (*c*) *judgment is rendered by his fellow-vassals and not by the king;* (*d*) *procedure is informal, but precedents are cited and law is being made.*

[The bishop of Durham was accused by the king of disloyalty and his lands were seized. After much argument it was agreed that a trial should be held at Salisbury. The bishop came, but pleaded clerical privilege].

The bishop said: "Lord barons and laymen . . . I will answer to the archbishops and bishops; I have nothing to say to you and I have not come here to receive your judgment. . . ." Then Roger Bigot [a great baron] said to the king: "You should tell the bishop why you accuse him, and if he will answer, we will judge him on his an-

[1] From the *Opera* of Simeon of Durham, ed. T. Arnold (London, 1882), vol. I, pp. 180-185.

swer; if not, do what your barons advise." The bishop answered: "I have said, and I repeat, that I totally reject the judgment of laymen. . . ." Then Hugh de Beaumont [another great baron], rising by order of the king, said to the bishop: "The king accuses you of this, that when his enemies were advancing on him . . . he summoned you, in my hearing, to come to his aid, and you promised that you would come with seven knights. . . . Instead you fled from the court . . . and so failed him in his hour of need. . . ." The bishop replied: "Hugh, say what you will; I won't answer you today. . . ." Hugh de Beaumont said: "If I cannot judge you today . . . then you and the other clergy shall never again judge me." [Lanfranc, archbishop of Canterbury, who was something of a legal expert, suggested that the bishop leave the room while the court decided whether he must answer]. When the bishop returned, Thomas archbishop of York said: "Lord bishop, our lord the archbishop and the king's court have judged that you must satisfy the king before you can regain your fief. . . ." [The bishop made another long argument against being judged by laymen and against being deprived of his *bishopric*. He asked to be allowed to take counsel with the other bishops. Lanfranc made the obvious reply: "The bishops are judges and so you cannot have them as your counsel." The bishop of Durham again complained that he was being deprived of his bishopric contrary to Church law.] Lanfranc answered: "We are not passing judgment on your bishopric but on your fief, and in this fashion we judged the bishop of Bayeux[2] before the father of the present king concerning the fief which he held. . . . The bishop said: "Lord archbishop, I have never mentioned a fief today . . . but I have complained about losing my bishopric. . . ." The archbishop replied: "If I haven't heard you speak of a fief, I still know that you hold a great one, and we will judge you on that." [The bishop gave notice that he would appeal to Rome, and was sent out again while the court formulated its de-

[2] Odo, bishop of Bayeux, half-brother of William the Conqueror, was accused of denying his brother the services of his knights in 1082. He was judged as an earl, not as a bishop, and he forfeited his fief, the county of Kent.

cision.] When the bishop returned . . . Hugh de Beaumont said: "Lord bishop, the king's court and these barons judge thus—since you will not answer the king on the charges which he made against you . . . you have forfeited your fief."

— Reading No. 25 —

THE DUKE OF NORMANDY AND THE PEACE OF GOD, 1135[1]

William the Conqueror had already enforced many provisions of the Peace of God, such as forbidding the burning of houses or attacks on merchants.[2] His son Henry in this document takes full responsibility for enforcing the Peace. The Church's part in originating the Peace is recognized by a payment to the bishop.

Henry, king of the English to . . . all faithful sons of Holy Church in Normandy, greeting. Know that in the presence of Hugh, archbishop of Rouen, and the bishops John of Lisieux, Audin of Evreux, John of Séez and Algar of Coutances, and by the common advice and consent of all my barons listed below, it has been decided and determined concerning manslayers who kill men contrary to the rules of the Truce and Peace of the Church, namely: If anyone wishes to accuse such a manslayer and challenge him to a judicial duel, the duel shall be held in my court. If the accused loses, the bishop in whose diocese this takes place shall have his fine of nine pounds from the goods of the convicted man by the hands of my judge. . . . If no one wishes to challenge the manslayer

[1] From *Le Très Ancien Coutumier de Normandie,* ed. E. J. Tardif (Rouen, 1881), pp. 65-68.

[2] C. H. Haskins, *Norman Institutions* (Cambridge, 1925), p. 283.

to a duel, the accused shall clear himself in the church of God by the agency and through the judgment of the Church.[3] If he is convicted there . . . the same thing shall be done about a fine to the bishop. . . . And if any manslayer . . . makes peace with me, the fine to the bishop shall not be included in the arrangements, but he must pay the bishop or make a separate peace with him. Witnesses: [9 barons]. Done at Rouen in the year of grace 1135.

[3] This would probably be done through compurgation: the accused would take an oath that he was innocent, and a fixed number of men would have to swear that they believed his oath.

— Reading No. 26 —

CEREMONY OF BECOMING A VASSAL, 1127[1]

This is one of the most complete descriptions we have of the forms used when a man became a vassal. Feudalism was fully developed by this time. Also, the feudal lords of Flanders had just accepted a new count (William Clito) after a disputed succession. It was important for William to be very careful to use the fullest and most binding forms in securing the allegiance of his new vassals. Notice that homage and fidelity, while closely associated, are rendered in separate acts.

✓ ✓ ✓

. . . On Thursday, homages were again done to the count. First, they did homage in this way. The count asked [the vassal] if he wished to become his man without reserve, and the latter answered: "I do." Then joining his hands together, he placed them in the hands of the count, and they bound themselves together by a kiss. In the second place, the man who had just done homage pledged fidelity . . . to the count in these words: "I promise on my faith to be faithful from now on to count William and to observe [the obligations of] my homage completely, in good faith, and without deceit, against all men," and this he swore on the relics of the saints. . . . Finally, with a little stick which he held in his hand, the count gave investiture [of fiefs] to all those who had . . . promised security, done homage, and taken the oath.

[1] *De Multro . . . Karoli comitis Flandriarum* by Galbert of Bruges, ed. H. Pirenne (Paris, 1891), p. 89.

— Reading No. 27 —

FEUDALISM IN GERMANY: EDICT OF THE EMPEROR CONRAD II, 1037[1]

Feudalism had developed more slowly in Germany than in France. The emperor could still intervene directly in disputes between great lords and their vassals. As in France, the knights desired to make their fiefs hereditary, but the opposition of the lords to this practice had been more effective in Germany than in the West. Conrad wanted the support of the knights in order to weaken some of the great lords; this edict favors the lesser vassals, though it still does not permit succession through females.

1) . . . We firmly order that no knight of a bishop, abbot, count or margrave . . . who now holds, or who has held and lost unjustly, a fief [benefice] from our lands or those of the Church . . . shall lose his fief without clear and manifest fault, and in accordance with the laws of our ancestors and the judgment of his peers.

2) If there is contention between lords and knights, even if the peers judge that the knight should lose his fief, if the knight says that the sentence was unjust and caused by prejudice, he shall keep his fief until he and his lord, with his peers, come before our court where the case will be decided justly. . . .

3) . . . When a knight dies . . . his son shall have the fief. If he has no son, but leaves a grandson born of a son, the grandson shall have the fief. . . . If he leaves

[1] *M. G. H., Leges,* Sect. IV, vol. 1 (Berlin, 1893), p. 90.

no such grandson, but has a legitimate brother on his father's side and if this brother . . . wishes to be vassal of the lord, he shall have the fief. . . .

4) Moreover, we absolutely forbid any lord to exchange or alter the character of a fief of his vassals without their consent. . . .

— Reading No. 28 —

MINISTERIALS IN TWELFTH-CENTURY GERMANY[1]

Ministerials were serfs who acted as officials (estate managers, stewards, etc.) and often as knights for their lords. In France they either remained peasants (village heads and the like) or were quickly absorbed into the class of knights. But in Germany they remained a distinct class into the thirteenth century. They improved their status steadily, as these documents show. Most of them were eventually recognized as the equals of free knights (which made them noble); some of them became counts or princes.

✓ ✓ ✓

Rules for the dependents of the monastery of Limburg, 1035.

Each man owes a shilling a year, each woman sixpence a year or a day's work once a week in the abbot's house. The abbot can assign unmarried sons to whatever service he likes, such as the kitchen or the mill. . . . Married men . . . as the abbot orders, may be keepers of grain or toll-collectors or foresters. If the abbot wishes . . . to make someone in his service a steward or a butler or a knight and gives him a benefice (fief) he shall keep it as long as he behaves well to the abbot. . . . A woman

[1] From *Ausgewählte Urkunden,* ed. W. Altmann and E. Bernheim (Berlin, 1895), pp. 140, 143, 148-153.

who marries outside the [abbot's] village . . . shall pay sixpence.[2]

The rules for the ministerials of Bamberg, c. 1060.

If a ministerial does not have a benefice from the bishop . . . and cannot obtain one, he may serve anyone he wishes, not as a dependent but as a free man. . . . If [a man with a benefice dies] and has a son, he shall have the benefice of his father; if not, the nearest relative on the father's side shall offer his lord his best hauberk (chain-mail shirt) or his best horse, and receive the benefice. In case of war, he must go to his lord at his own expense; afterwards he serves at the lord's expense. If the army goes to Italy,[3] the lord should give each man with a hauberk a horse and three pounds. . . . These men can be made to serve their lord in only five offices—as stewards or butlers or chamberlains or marshals or huntsmen.

The rights of the ministerials of Cologne, c. 1154.

. . . All ministerials of Cologne, with benefices or without, must help their lord the archbishop defend his land. . . . If the archbishop for any reason becomes offended with one of his ministerials . . . and seizes his land, the ministerial shall ask the nobles of the land and especially those who are called high officials of the court, . . . to intercede for him. If he cannot regain the archbishop's favor within a year . . . he may go and serve another lord. . . . The ministerials are bound to go with their lord the archbishop on expeditions across the Alps for the coronation of the emperor,[3] especially those who have property yielding 5 marks or more in income. . . . The archbishop shall give each of them 10 marks to arm themselves, and 40 ells of cloth . . . to clothe their servants . . . and one pack-horse for each two knights. . . . When they come to the Alps, each knight should be paid one mark a month from then on. . . . [If he is

[2] Payment for permission to marry outside the village was a mark of serfdom.

[3] The emperor usually met opposition when he went to Italy to be crowned by the pope. He always took an army with him, made up largely of contingents furnished by bishops and abbots.

not paid] he may lawfully go home without loss of honor or of lands. . . . The nobles of the territory of Cologne, who have justice over their lands, have no right to judge the ministerials of the archbishop. . . . The eldest son of a ministerial shall receive his father's benefice when his father dies. . . . [A younger son] may offer himself to his lord as a knight and ministerial and promise fidelity and service, and if the lord accepts him . . . and he serves well for a year . . . he is bound to be given a benefice. . . . If the lord does not receive him . . . he may go where he will and serve whom he will. . . . If there is war between the [new] lord and the archbishop, the knight . . . does not have to abandon his [new] lord. . . .

— Reading No. 29 —

MINISTERIALS IN THE COUNTY OF HAINAUT, c. 1195[1]

In the Low Countries as in Germany, the class of ministerials remained important up to the thirteenth century. Hainaut (now part of Belgium) was under strong French influence, but its feudal institutions developed more slowly. Ministerials are still distinguished from nobles even though they serve in the count's council and army. (This distinction is erased during the next century.) And the count still rewards his followers with horses, fine clothes, and money rather than with fiefs.

Expert knights, many of them nobles and some of them ministerials, were the special councillors . . . and companions in arms of the lord count Baldwin of Hainaut. . . . Some were councillors only, some were companions in arms, and some were both. The councillors were [6 names]. Councillors and companions in arms were [10 names]. Companions in arms and occasional councillors were [29 names]. The count honored all these with gifts of horses and armor and clothes and money, and some of them he enriched at the cost of greater benefices [possibly fiefs].

[1] From the *Chronicon Hanoniense* of Gislebertus of Mons, ed. G. H. Pertz (Hannover, 1869), pp. 289-290.

— Reading No. 30 —

KNIGHTS' FEES IN ENGLAND, 1166[1]

In both England and Normandy the amount of service owed by vassals had been carefully specified by William the Conqueror. (See Reading No. 23.) *Henry II sought even greater precision. In 1166 in England and in 1172 in Normandy he asked his immediate vassals to give him the names of all their knights. Thus he could learn whether they had enough knights to meet their quota or whether they had surplus knights (which might be an excuse for increasing payments of scutage or relief). He could also insist that all knights pledge fealty to him. This was part of the process of systematizing feudalism, which was especially strong in England and Normandy.*

Return of John, count of Eu

To Henry, king of England, duke of Normandy and Aquitaine and count of Anjou, John count of Eu sends greeting. Know that I have in the district of Hastings, by old enfieffments of the time of king Henry, your grandfather, 56 knights. But my father used to have 60 [2] knights there . . . of whom the bishopric of Chichester now has four and you receive the service [of these four] from the bishopric. The names of those owing the 56 knights

[1] From *Liber Niger Scaccarii,* ed. Thomas Hearne (London, 1774), pp. 66-67, 133-134.

[2] William, whenever possible, assigned quotas of knight service in multiples of five. This was probably because a basic military unit was the constabulary, a group of ten knights.

are . . . [12 men, of whom two owe 10 knights, two 7 knights, etc.] In addition, I have on my domains men owing the service of 6½ knights, whose names are . . . [8 in all]. I have no newly enfieffed knight.

Letter of the Lord Bishop of Coventry.[3]

To his venerable lord Henry, king of England etc., Richard, by the grace of God humble bishop of the church of Coventry sends greeting and God's blessing. Sheriff Stephen asked us, venerable lord, on your behalf, how many of the knights which we owe you were enfieffed in the time of king Henry, your grandfather, and how many were enfieffed after his death and if some of the number is charged to our domain.[4] He also ordered us to send a written list of their names to your majesty. . . .

Their names are . . . [21 in all, holding 13⅜ fees. Only one owes the service of two knights, 6 owe half a knight, and three a quarter of a knight, i.e., 20 days' or 10 days' service when a knight does 40 days' service. Breaking up of fiefs has gone much further here than in the lands of the count of Eu]. These named were enfieffed in the time of King Henry, your grandfather.

After his death were enfieffed . . . [6 in all, holding at most half a knight's fee and as little as a seventh. The total is a little more than 1⅓ fees].

We have no knight's fee charged to our domain beyond the 15 knights which we owe you. But whatever is lacking from this number,[4] we are accustomed to make up from our treasury [by paying scutage].

[3] In England and in Normandy most of the bishops and many abbots and abbesses owed military service. This was an important source of strength to the king, for he appointed these men and they were usually loyal to him.

[4] As can be seen, the fractions do not add up to exactly 15, and it is likely that some of the lesser fiefholders never gave actual service. The bishop probably had paid scutage instead of furnishing knights for many years.

— Reading No. 31 —

THE FRANCHISE THEORY OF FEUDAL JUSTICE[1]

In their efforts to make feudalism more systematic and to extend their control over courts of lesser lords, great lords developed the franchise theory of justice: that is, no one had the right to hold a court except through delegation of power from a superior. This was bad history, but useful as a political device. The idea appeared very early in Anglo-Norman law.

The first quotation comes from the Leges Henrici Primi, *an unofficial treatise on law written between 1114 and 1118 by a clerk at the court of Henry I of England. The second comes from a statement of ducal rights in Normandy acknowledged by a group of barons about 1172-1174.*

✓ ✓ ✓

The king has justice over all the lands which he has in his domain. He can make manors out of these lands and give them [to a vassal] with complete or shared rights of justice. He can also give manors but keep the justice for himself. For the king's rights of justice do not necessarily go with the gift of a manor, rather they are a personal (and separate) grant.

✓ ✓ ✓

[1] The first selection is from *Die Gesetze der Angelsachsen,* ed. F. Lieberman, vol. I (Halle, 1903), pp. 559-60. The second is from *Le très ancien coutumier de Normandie,* ed. E. J. Tardif (Rouen, 1881), pp. 64-65.

. . . These cases belong to the sword of the Duke [i.e., are part of the Duke's rights of government]: homicide, whether done secretly . . . or openly—justice in this kind of case . . . belongs to the Duke alone or to those to whom he or his ancestors gave it. In the same way, cutting off or breaking a man's limbs, . . . robbery . . . rape . . . arson . . . premeditated assault, assault inside a house, assault on [a peasant at] a plow, assault on the king's highway,[2] assault on one going to the king's court,[2] . . . breaking of truces made before royal judges,[2] and all pleas concerning military service or coinage belong to the Duke alone.

[2] The Duke of Normandy was also king of England, so the king's highways, courts, and judges referred to here are actually ducal highways, etc. None of these terms refers to the king of France.

— Reading No. 32 —

PROTECTION OF REAR-VASSALS BY THE KING IN ENGLAND, 1187, 1202[1]

The first quotation states the general rule, established by 1187, forbidding lords to proceed against their vassals without a royal writ. Most of these writs had the effect of moving the case to a royal court. One very popular royal writ established the procedure of novel disseisin, *by which a jury was asked whether the plaintiff had been dispossessed without due process of law. The second document shows this writ being used in 1202 to protect a rear-vassal against a baron. Note that in England these cases went directly to a royal court, while in France they were apt to be heard as appeals from the lords' courts.* (See Reading No. 33.)

✓ ✓ ✓

Moreover, it should be known that according to the custom of the kingdom no one is required to answer in the court of his lord concerning any of his fiefs without the writ of the lord king. . . .

✓ ✓ ✓

[1] The first quotation comes from *De legibus et consuetudinibus regni Angliae* by "Glanville," ed. G. E. Woodbine (New Haven, 1932), p. 157. The second is from *Select Civil Pleas,* ed. W. P. Baildon (Selden Society Publications III, London, 1890), vol. I, case no. 224.

The jury comes to answer whether Gilbert de Gaunt [a great baron] . . . has unjustly and without judgment disseised [dispossessed] William son of William of his fief in Barton: The jury says that he was so disseised. Judgment: Let William have possession of the fief. . . . Damage, one mark . . . and let Gilbert be amerced [fined] in London. . . .

— Reading No. 33 —

PROTECTION OF REAR-VASSALS IN THE COURT OF THE KING OF FRANCE, 1163, 1224[1]

In France, unlike England, the king could not bring all important cases directly before his judges. He could, however, protect subjects of great lords by hearing appeals from the lords' courts in his court.

In the first case a clerk is trying to appeal from the court of the abbot of St. Denis to the king. The abbot is unwilling to allow the appeal, and the clerk gets his patron, a cardinal, to intercede for him.

In the second case, the appeal is from the court of the countess of Flanders. She is accused of failure to do justice, which may mean simply that she failed to have the case heard in her court. She tries to have the case sent back to her court and fails. She then claims that she can be judged only by the peers of France (at this time six great lay lords and six bishops who held counties or duchies), and not by royal officers. This plea also fails, and the royal court hears the case.

✓ ✓ ✓

1163 A.D.

To the illustrious king of the French, Henry, cardinal priest of the Holy Roman church, greeting. . . . Our clerk Adam, believing that we have some influence with

[1] From *Textes relatifs a l'histoire du Parlement,* ed. Ch. V. Langlois (Paris, 1888), pp. 24, 35.

you, has humbly asked us to write you a letter. He says that, relying on your justice . . . he appealed to your court concerning a certain case about a house which was being heard . . . in the court of the lord abbot of St. Denis. . . . Because you were occupied with important affairs you sent a man of yours, Urric Trossevache [a member of the royal household], in your place, so that he could rapidly proceed to make a judgment. . . . The abbot, however, would not allow this agent of yours to be present at the trial. . . . Therefore, we beg you . . . for the love of God and ourselves . . . to be good enough to end the difficulties of this poor man.

1224 A.D.

Since there had been a dispute between Jeanne, countess of Flanders, and Jean de Néelle. . . . Jean appealed to the king's court against the countess for failure to do justice. . . . The countess claimed that Jean de Néelle had peers in Flanders by whom he ought to be judged in her court and that she was ready to do justice in her court through Jean's peers. . . . Jean de Néelle, on the other hand, said that he refused to go back to the countess's court under any conditions, because she had failed to do him justice and because he had appealed to the king's court about this failure. . . . It was judged . . . that the countess must answer him in the king's court. . . .

Moreover, since the peers of France claimed that . . . the officers of the king's household should not take part with them in a judgment as a peer of France, and the officers on the contrary said that according to the usage and customs of France they should be present . . . it was judged in the king's court that the officers of the king's household should be present with the peers to judge a peer, and then the said officers with the peers passed judgment on the countess of Flanders at Paris in the year of our Lord 1224.

— Reading No. 34B —

THE CONFISCATION OF KING JOHN'S FRENCH FIEFS, 1202

This is the most famous example of the confiscation of a fief by a lord. John, as duke of Normandy and Aquitaine and count of Anjou, was a vassal of king Philip of France. John was charged with various misdeeds by some of his vassals; when he gave them no satisfaction they appealed to John's lord, king Philip. (This is another example of protection of rear-vassals by the overlord.) John, summoned to Philip's court to answer the charges, failed to appear. The court ruled that he had forfeited his fiefs, and Philip enforced the ruling by a successful war.

✓ ✓ ✓

A. Account of an English Chronicler[1]

King John began to attack fiercely the count of La Marche . . . and his brother, the count of Eu, who had rebelled against him because [John had married] the daughter of the count of Angoulême, who had previously been betrothed to the count of La Marche. But since these counts could not long resist John's attack, they complained to king Philip as the chief lord. . . . King Philip many times ordered the king of England to cease his attack and make peace with his men. But when the

[1] From the *Chronicon Anglicanum* of Ralph of Coggeshall, ed. J. Stevenson (London, 1875), pp. 134-135. Ralph was an unusually well-informed chronicler.

king of England refused to listen to the pleas and orders of the king of France, he was summoned by the barons of the kingdom of France, in his capacity as count of Anjou and duke of Aquitaine, to come to the court of his lord, the king of France, at Paris and to accept the judgment of the court. . . . The king of England, however, replied that as duke of Normandy he was not bound to come to Paris. . . . King Philip, in reply, said it was scarcely just that he should lose his rights over Aquitaine because the duke of Normandy and the duke of Aquitaine were the same person. . . . Finally, the court of the king of France judged that the king of England should lose all the land which he had held of the king of France, because for a long time he had failed almost completely to give the service owed for these lands, and because he would not obey any commands of his lord.

B. Letter of Louis VIII to the Burgesses and Consuls of Limoges, May, 1224[2]

Louis, by the grace of God king of the French, to his beloved consuls and all the burgesses of Limoges, greeting. Let all of you know that John, former king of England, was deprived forever of all the land which he held on this side of the Channel from our dear father Philip, formerly king of the French, by the common and unanimous judgment of the peers and other barons of France . . . and all that land fell under the rightful domination of our father. . . .

[2] From *Etude sur la vie et le règne de Louis VIII* by Ch. Petit-Dutaillis (Paris, 1894), p. 516. The letter was written to explain to the burgesses of Limoges why they now owed military service to the king of France.

— Reading No. 35 —

FINANCIAL ASPECTS OF FEUDALISM: SCUTAGE AND AIDS[1]

The two documents below illustrate Anglo-Norman customs of the late twelfth century. The first was written about 1179, as part of a treatise on the Exchequer (the English accounting office). Notice that it says plainly that the king prefers mercenaries to vassals. The second document comes from a book on Norman law written about the middle of the thirteenth century, but most of it is a repetition of earlier texts. Both documents show how money could be made out of the feudal relationship.

✓ ✓ ✓

Occasionally, when enemies threaten or attack the kingdom, the king orders that a certain sum be paid from each knight's fee [a fief which could support a knight], such as one mark or one pound [a mark was two-thirds of a pound] to provide wages or bonuses for soldiers. For the king prefers to expose mercenaries rather than his own people to the chances of war. This payment, because it is reckoned according to the number of shields [each knight owed is a "shield"], is called shield-money [scutage].

✓ ✓ ✓

[1] The first document comes from *Select Charters,* ed. W. Stubbs, ninth edition (Oxford, 1921), p. 218. The second is from the *Summa de legibus Normannie,* ed. E. J. Tardif (Rouen and Paris, 1896), pp. 110-111.

There are three principal aids in Normandy: the first for promoting the eldest son of the lord to the rank of knight, the second for marrying the eldest daughter of the lord, the third for redeeming the body of the lord from prison when he has been captured fighting for the duke of Normandy. These aids in some fiefs equal half the value of a relief and in some fiefs a third.[2]

[2] According to the same law-book (p. 107), relief in Normandy was 15 pounds for a knight's fee and 100 pounds for a barony. Note that the Norman pound was worth only about one-fourth of the English pound.

— Reading No. 36 —

FINANCIAL ASPECTS OF FEUDALISM: RELIEF, WARDSHIP, AND MARRIAGE[1]

The quotations below come from an early book on English law, written by an official of King Henry II about 1187. It should be remembered that English law was especially strict on these matters. There was no relief in most of Germany and in some parts of France. Few other rulers were able to exploit their rights of wardship and marriage as successfully as the king of England. As the notes show, Magna Carta attempted to limit some of these abuses.

When a male heir of full age is left [by a deceased vassal] he shall remain in possession of his inheritance . . . as long as he has offered his lord homage in the presence of respectable men, and a reasonable relief. It is said that by the custom of the kingdom a reasonable relief for one knight's fee is five pounds. . . . For a barony, however, there is no certain rule, because the chief barons must satisfy the king about their reliefs according to his will and mercy.[2]

[1] From *De legibus et consuetudinibus regni Angliae,* by "Glanville," ed. G. E. Woodbine (New Haven, 1932), pp. 127-128, 107, 109.

[2] Magna Carta in ch. 2 fixed the relief for a barony at 100 pounds and for a knight's fee "at most" at five pounds.

If the heirs are minors, then they shall remain under the wardship of their lords until they are of age . . . which is 21 in the case of the son and heir of a knight. . . . Lords have full powers during wardship over the persons and possessions of heirs of their men—for example, in granting churches which are part of the fief, or in marrying off girls who are in wardship. . . . Even if a female heir is of age, she shall remain in the wardship of her lord until she is married according to the desire and with the consent of the lord. . . . And if a girl . . . marries without the consent of her lord, by the just law and custom of the realm she shall lose her inheritance. . . .[3]

[3] Magna Carta, chs. 4 and 5, forbids guardians to despoil the lands of their wards. In chs. 6 and 8 the lord is required to find a suitable husband for a female ward and is forbidden to force widows to remarry.

— Reading No. 37 —

SALE OF RIGHTS OF MARRIAGE BY JOHN, 1207[1]

The following extracts come from the Pipe Roll—that is, the accounts rendered by sheriffs—of 1207. John is using his right as feudal lord to control marriages of heiresses of his vassals as a way of making money. Notice that a woman may avoid an undesirable marriage by bribing the king.

Thomas of Whitchurch gives 100 marks and two palfreys to have as his wife Margaret Lestrange who was wife of Thomas Noel, with her inheritance, her marriage portion and her dower.

Fulk FitzWarin owes 1200 marks . . . and two palfreys to have as his wife the daughter of Robert Vavasseur, that is, Matilda, with her inheritance.

Matilda, who was wife of Hugh Wake, offers 20 marks that she may not be forced to marry again.

Quenild, daughter of Richard FitzRoger, owes 60 marks and two palfreys that she may be allowed to marry whomever she pleases, with the advice of her friends, as long as she marries no one who is an enemy of the king.

[1] From *The Great Roll of the Pipe for the Ninth Year of King John,* ed. A. M. Kirkus (London, 1946), pp. 6, 110, 154, 163.

— Reading No. 38 —

A MONEY-FIEF, 1103[1]

This agreement between Henry I of England and Count Robert II of Flanders is one of the earliest known examples of a money-fief. Henry is trying to secure a formidable addition to his army. It is doubtful if William the Conqueror had more than 5000 to 6000 soldiers of all kinds at Hastings, and Robert promises 1000 knights. The price is a sum equal to the royal revenues of an average English county.

The document also illustrates the problems of multiple homage. Although Robert's chief lord is the king of France, from whom he holds Flanders, he agrees to give as little help to the king of France as possible, and to devote his main efforts to aiding his secondary lord, the king of England.

Robert count of Flanders pledges to king Henry by faith and oath . . . that he will help him to hold and defend the kingdom of England against all men who can live and die, saving his fidelity to Philip, king of France. If king Philip plans to attack king Henry in England, count Robert, if he can, will persuade king Philip to stay at home. . . . And if king Philip shall invade England and shall bring count Robert with him, the count shall bring as few men with him as he can do without forfeiting his fief to the king of France.

[1] From *Actes des comtes de Flandre,* ed. F. Vercauteren (Brussels, 1938), no. 30.

. . . After count Robert is summoned by the king of England, he shall get a thousand knights together as quickly as possible in his ports, ready to cross to England. And the king shall find . . . enough ships for these knights, each knight having three horses.

. . . And if king Henry wishes count Robert to help him in Normandy or in Maine . . . the count shall come there with a thousand knights and shall aid king Henry faithfully, as his ally and lord from whom he holds a fief. . . . And if at this time, king Philip shall attack king Henry in Normandy, count Robert shall go with king Philip with only twenty knights, and all his other knights shall remain with king Henry. . . .

The king promises to protect count Robert in life and limb, . . . and to assure him against the loss of all his land . . . as long as the count shall hold to these agreements. And in return for these agreements and this service king Henry will give as a fief to count Robert 500 pounds of English money every year. . . .

— Reading No. 39 —

MULTIPLE HOMAGE, EARLY THIRTEENTH CENTURY[1]

By the early thirteenth century the problem of homage had become even more complicated than in the twelfth. John of Toul has four lords. The two most important are the count of Champagne and the count of Grandpré. He has done liege homage to both, though his homage to Grandpré takes precedence over his homage to Champagne. But he will try to satisfy both lords if he can.

I, John of Toul, make it known that I am the liege man of Lady Beatrice, countess of Troyes and of her son, my dearest lord count Thibaud of Champagne, against all persons, living or dead, except for the liege homage I have done to lord Enguerran of Coucy, lord John of Arcis, and the count of Grandpré. If it should happen that the count of Grandpré should be at war with the countess and count of Champagne for his own personal grievances, I will personally go to the assistance of the count of Grandpré and will send to the countess and count of Champagne, if they summon me, the knights I owe for the fief which I hold of them. But if the count of Grandpré shall make war on the countess and count of Champagne on behalf of his friends and not for his own personal grievances, I shall serve in person with the

[1] From the *Glossarium* of Du Cange, under the word "ligius" (vol. IV, p. 203 of the 1733 edition).

countess and count of Champagne and I will send one knight to the count of Grandpré to give the service owed from the fief which I hold of him. But I will not myself invade the territory of the count of Grandpré. . . .

— Reading No. 40 —

LORDS AND KNIGHTS IN FRENCH EPIC POETRY[1]

From the late eleventh century into the thirteenth, French poets produced many epic poems which were recited at the courts of great lords and other gatherings. These poems, composed to please audiences of feudal lords and knights, naturally exaggerate the wealth, power, and fighting ability of the feudal class. On the other hand, when they mention without any reproof examples of bad temper and bad manners, we can feel reasonably sure that men of the period thought this was natural behavior. In their earliest form these epics (or chansons de geste*) came from the pre-chivalric age, and they remained popular for several generations after chivalric ideas had begun to permeate the upper classes.*

The most famous (and perhaps earliest) of these poems is the Song of Roland. *I have chosen, however, to use as an example of this type of work extracts from* Raoul de Cambrai. *An early version of* Raoul *is almost as old as the* Roland, *and even the fuller version which I have used seems full of archaic traits. It illustrates some of the problems of the early vassal-lord relationship, and it demonstrates better than the* Roland *the extreme violence and lack of self-restraint of some feudal lords.*

✓ ✓ ✓

[1] From *Raoul de Cambrai,* pub. by P. Meyer and A. Longnon (Paris, 1882). There is a good English translation by Jessie Crosland (London, 1926).

[Raoul's father, count of Cambrai, died just before Raoul was born. The king gave the county to one of his faithful vassals. When Raoul came of age, he demanded his father's inheritance. The king recognized that Raoul had a claim, but could not dispossess a powerful lord. Instead, he rashly promised Raoul the land of the next count who died. Unfortunately, at this point Herbert, count of Vermandois, died, leaving several sons to succeed him. The king tried to keep Raoul from claiming Vermandois, without success. Raoul's mother also tried to persuade him to wait for a better occasion. He answered her roughly, as most heroes of the *chansons de geste* did when women interfered with men's business:]

"Curse that nobleman—and I count him a coward—who listens to a lady's advice when he ought to fight. Go to your rooms and loll around there. Drink something to fatten your belly. And think only about eating and drinking for you have no business with other things."

[Raoul marches on Vermandois and camps near the convent of Origny. The abbess, before she took the veil, had been the mistress of a member of the Vermandois family and had born a son, Bernier, who was Raoul's squire and had recently been knighted by him. She asked her son why he was making war on Vermandois. He answered:]

"I would not do this for all the wealth of Baghdad. My lord Raoul is more evil than Judas. But—he is my lord. He gives me horses and clothing, ornaments and silk from the East. I will not desert him, for all the wealth of Damascus until everyone says: 'Bernier, you have just cause.' " "Son," said his mother, "by my faith, you are right. Serve your lord and you will gain God's blessing."

[Raoul promises to spare Origny, but a brawl arises and his men burn the town and convent. All the nuns, including Bernier's mother, die in the flames. Bernier still serves Raoul, but is deeply troubled. He reproaches Raoul, who says:]

"Bastard and traitor, only God and a sense of pity have kept me from cutting you to pieces. Why shouldn't I destroy you now?"

Bernier said: "This is fine friendship! I have served you and loved you and aided you in every way. This is poor payment for my good service. . . . I will fight anyone who calls me a bastard or renegade. And you yourself wouldn't dare touch me. . . ."

When Raoul heard this . . . he seized a great lance . . . and in fury struck Bernier so that his head was broken and blood ran down.

[Raoul realizes his fault and offers amends, but Bernier says he will never be reconciled with Raoul "until this red blood goes back to my head of its own accord." Various attempts are made to reconcile the two, but eventually Bernier gives the formal defiance which frees him from his oath of allegiance:]

"Lord Raoul, this argument is ended. . . . In return for all my service you treated me contemptibly. You burned my mother in the church of Origny and you struck me so that blood flowed down." He drew three hairs of the ermine (cloak) he was wearing through the links of his bright chain-mail. He threw them at Raoul and said: "Warrior, I defy you. Never say that I betrayed you."

[Bernier joins the army of Vermandois and battle begins. Here the poet's imagination runs wild; there are thousands of knights on each side; helmets and shields are ornamented with gold and jewels; Raoul strikes off the heads of more than twenty men. In the end, pride causes his downfall. He had cut off the hand of Ernaut, a Vermandois lord, and was pursuing him in order to kill him. Ernaut begged for mercy, but Raoul said:]

"Make ready for your end. This sword shall part your head from your body. Nothing can help you now. Neither God nor man nor all the saints can save you."

These words did great harm to Raoul, for by them he denied the power of God. Ernaut heard them and took courage. He rebuked Raoul: "By God, Raoul, you are a real heathen, full of pride, of wickedness and of presumption. You are no better than a mad dog, since you have denied God and his love. . . . For the God of glory can save me, if he takes pity on me."

[Ernaut then turns to fight, but Bernier comes to rescue him. Bernier makes one more plea for peace, but Raoul threatens to kill him.]

When Bernier saw . . . that his plea was useless, he rushed at Raoul and Raoul spurred his horse toward him. Each struck a great blow on the other's shield so that both splintered beneath the buckles [by which they were held]. . . . Then Raoul struck Bernier such a blow that he would have been killed . . . if God and justice had not been on his side. . . . Then, in great anger, Bernier struck Raoul on his shining helmet. Flowers and precious stones flew through the air and the blow went right through the cap of chain-mail into the brain. . . . Raoul fell from his horse . . . struggled to rise, and with a great effort drew his sword. But he cannot tell where to strike and his arm sinks to the ground. . . . Bernier began to weep . . . and said: "I no longer seek vengeance." But Ernaut said . . . "I have my hand to avenge". . . . He struck him a pitiless blow on the helmet . . . and then plunged his sword into the heart. Then the soul of the noble knight left his body. May God receive it, if we dare pray for him.

— Reading No. 41 —

A TOURNAMENT IN 1177[1]

This story comes from the life of William the Marshal, written by a French minstrel at the request of William's son. William was one of the most famous knights of his day and the faithful supporter of Henry II, Richard, and John. He became earl of Pembroke and was Regent of England after John's death in 1216.

Tournaments became fashionable in the twelfth century as a substitute for the private wars which were being outlawed by strong rulers. As this passage shows, early tournaments were rather disorganized; a group of knights met another group and fought in any way that pleased them, single combat or group actions. The mock battle might range over a wide space, though those who wished to please the ladies probably tried to do some fighting within their view.

William heard that there was to be a notable tournament of great barons at Joigny. . . . He and his companions came to the castle of Joigny . . . armed themselves there, and then went down to a pleasant meadow outside the town. . . . There they were told that they had too many men and the other side too few . . . so they dismounted and waited, fully armed, for their adversaries.

[1] From *L'histoire de Guillaume le Maréchal,* ed. Paul Meyer (Paris, 1891), vol. I, pp. 125-129. There is a good life of William Marshal, which paraphrases much of the poem, by Sidney Painter (Baltimore, 1933).

Then the countess of Joigny came forth . . . with her ladies and damsels, elegantly dressed, and as beautiful as they could be. . . . The knights . . . were delighted by the arrival of the ladies . . . and one of them said: "Let us dance while we wait and we won't be so bored." They took each other's hands and then another knight asked: "Who will be kind enough to sing for us? William . . . then began to sing . . . which pleased everyone there. . . . When he had finished his song . . . a minstrel, who had just been made a herald-of-arms, sang a new song . . . of which the refrain was: "Marshal, please give me a good horse." When the Marshal heard this . . . he left the dance without a word . . . and a squire brought him his horse. . . . The other party of knights was approaching, . . . the Marshal rode at one of them, confident of his prowess, and with his strong and powerful lance knocked his opponent off his horse. . . . Then he had the minstrel mount it . . . and the minstrel rode back to those who were still dancing and said: "See what a good horse the Marshal gave me!". . . . Then, as they saw the other group of knights, they put on their helmets and closed their vizors. . . . Those who had been dancing with the ladies strove with body, heart, and soul to distinguish themselves, and they did so well that everyone was astonished.

— Reading No. 42 —

JUDGMENT BY KNIGHTS, c. 1200[1]

This quotation, from the earliest treatise on Norman law, illustrates the important position of knights in twelfth-century law-courts. They acted as judges, under the presidency of and with the advice of royal officials, but the final responsibility was theirs.

Assizes [district-courts] are held by barons and law-abiding men. Each man should be judged by his equal: thus barons and knights who know the details of the law and who fear God, may judge each other, and the people subject to them. But a peasant or a common man may not judge a knight or a member of the clergy. . . .

Three or four knights, or barons, are chosen to hold assizes. They are sworn to give lawful justice, to preserve the rights of the innocent, to keep records faithfully, and to take no presents from wicked men to oppress the innocent.

[1] From *Le très ancien coutumier de Normandie,* ed. E. J. Tardif (Rouen, 1881), pp. 24-25.

— Reading No. 43 —

THE CHURCH AND THE KNIGHTS[1]

The increasing social and political importance of the knight is illustrated by the development of special ceremonies by which knighthood was conferred. This would not have been necessary in the ninth or tenth century. Furthermore, the church began to recognize the importance of knighthood by taking part in these ceremonies. The practice seems to have started in the eleventh century, but was just beginning to become common in the twelfth.

This selection is taken from a book on politics, written in 1159 by John of Salisbury, a great twelfth-century scholar, friend of Thomas Becket, and eventually bishop of Chartres.

✓ ✓ ✓

Knights rightfully have many privileges. . . . They are freer [than other men] and they enjoy many privileges. . . . There is no knight who is not bound to the church by a tacit or express oath. . . . And now a solemn custom has grown up, that on the day when a man is girt with the belt of knighthood, he goes solemnly to a church, places his sword on the altar like an offering . . . and, as it were dedicates himself to the altar and promises to God the service of his sword. . . . Thus when knights offer their sword, and . . . redeem the first token of their

[1] From the *Policraticus* of John of Salisbury, ed. C. C. I. Webb (Oxford, 1909) book VI, ch. 10.

rank from the altar, they bind themselves to the perpetual service of the Church. They can do much for the church, but must not do anything against it. . . . For the military arm falls easily into violence and is accustomed to plunder other men's property. . . .

— Reading No. 44 —

THE KNIGHT BECOMES A COURTIER[1]

This description of the ideal knight comes from part 1 of the Romance of the Rose, *an allegory written by Guillaume de Lorris about 1237. This was one of the most popular poems of the Middle Ages; hundreds of manuscript copies still exist. Notice that the author stresses acceptable social behavior; even military skill is desirable only because it enhances a knight's standing at court.*

But be thou careful to possess
Thy soul in gentleness and grace,
Kindly of heart and bright of face
Towards all men, be they great or small. . . .
Watch well thy lips, that they may be
Ne'er stained with ill-timed ribaldry. . . .

Have special care
To honor dames as thou dost fare
Thy worldly ways, and shouldst thou hear
Calumnious speech of them, no fear
Have thou to bid men hold their peace. . . .
Let him who would in love succeed
To courteous word wed noble deed.

[1] From the *Romance of the Rose* of Guillaume de Lorris, trans. by F. S. Ellis (London, 1900), vol. I, lines 2184-2291.

And next remember that, above
All else, gay heart inspireth love.
If thou shouldst know some cheerful play
Or game to wile dull hours away
My counsel is, neglect it not. . . .
And much with ladies 'twill advance
Thy suit, if well thou break a lance.
For who in arms his own doth hold
Winneth acceptance manifold.
And if a voice strong, sweet and clear
Thou hast, and dames desire to hear
Thee sing, seek not to make excuse.

— Reading No. 45 —

ORDINANCE OF PHILIP AUGUSTUS OF FRANCE, 1190[1]

Philip issued this ordinance just before he left France on the Third Crusade. It includes our first description of the duties of a bailli. *These men had extensive powers in local government, but were closely supervised by the king and could be removed by him. The first* baillis *were probably instituted a few years before 1190; they remained the chief agents of royal authority in the provinces for two centuries. They were strong enough to control feudal lords, but too dependent on the king to become lords themselves.*

First, we order our *baillis* to establish in each of our towns four prudent, law-abiding and respectable men; no business of the town shall be transacted without the advice of at least two of them. . . .

And we establish *baillis* in each of our lands, who shall fix a day called an assize each month in their *bailliages*. On this day all those who have complaints shall receive justice without delay, and we shall have our rights and justice. . . .

Moreover, we order that our dearest mother, the queen, and our beloved and faithful uncle, William archbishop

[1] From *Gesta Philippi Augusti* (ed. H. F. Delaborde, Paris, 1882), pp. 100-102.

of Reims, shall hold a court at Paris every four months to hear the complaints of the men of our realm and to decide them for the glory of God and the welfare of the realm.

We also order that at these meetings . . . our *baillis* shall come before them and tell them of the affairs of our land.

If any of our *baillis* shall do wrong . . . we order the archbishop and the queen . . . to send us letters, telling which *bailli* has done wrong and what he did. . . . Then we, with the aid of God, shall punish them in such a way . . . that others may have good reason to be deterred.

— Reading No. 46 —

THE IDEAL *BAILLI* OF THE THIRTEENTH CENTURY[1]

This description of the ideal bailli *comes from an influential book on the law of northern France, written by Philippe de Beaumanoir. Beaumanoir had been a* bailli *himself for many years; he wrote this description about 1283. Compare Reading No. 45, written in 1190, to see how the office has developed.*

A man who wants to be a loyal and upright *bailli* should have ten virtues . . . of which the lady and mistress of all the others . . . is wisdom.

The second virtue is . . . that he should ardently love God our Father and Savior, and for the love of God, Holy Church. . . .

The third virtue is . . . that he should be kind and approachable . . . not to criminals . . . but to those who mean well and to the common people and in offenses caused more by bad luck than by malice. . . .

The fourth virtue is . . . that he should be patient and willing to listen . . . because a *bailli* who is in too much of a hurry . . . or . . . who is angered by what he hears, cannot well remember what is brought up before him in court. . . .

The fifth virtue is . . . that he should be courageous and vigorous, and not lazy. For the lazy *bailli* . . . has other men do things he should do himself. . . . And the

[1] From *Coutumes de Beauvaisis* by Philippe de Beaumanoir (ed. A. Salmon, Paris, 1899), vol. I, pp. 26-27.

cowardly *bailli* does not dare punish the rich man who has done something against the poor. . . .

The sixth virtue . . . is generosity. . . .

The seventh virtue is . . . that he should obey all the orders of his lord, except for orders which might endanger his soul if he carried them out. . . . And it is better for a *bailli* to resign . . . than to do wrong knowingly.

The eighth virtue . . . is to be well informed . . . about right and wrong, about the good and bad people [in his district] . . . about the wishes and habits of his lord and those of his council . . . and about his own followers . . . because a *bailli* who would do no wrong of his own accord may be disgraced by the misdeeds of his followers.

The ninth virtue . . . is that he should know how to make the most [of his lord's property] without doing wrong to others and that he should know how to keep accounts. . . . If he is a good *bailli* the income from his lord's land will increase. . . . And it is very important to know how to keep accounts, for one of the greatest dangers in the office of a *bailli* is to be negligent in his accounting. . . .

The tenth virtue . . . is the best of all, and without it none of the others are worth anything . . . even wisdom cannot exist without it. And this virtue is honesty. . . . Dishonesty can do more harm in a man who should maintain justice than in others . . . and a lord should immediately discharge a *bailli* as soon as he knows that he is dishonest. . . .

— Reading No. 47 —

CIRCUIT JUDGES IN ENGLAND[1]

Circuit judges had been used in England since the time of the Conquest for hearing specific cases. By the time of Henry II (1154-1189) they were given more general commissions and heard all criminal cases, many civil cases, and cases touching the king's rights. This checked the power of feudal lords and opened a career in government service to the upper clergy and royal vassals. The first extract describes the circuit judges as they were seen by a late twelfth-century chronicler, Ralph de Diceto. The second is a commission given to the circuit judges in 1221; similar commissions had been issued in the twelfth century.

[Speaking of Henry II, Ralph says:] The King was most intent on doing justice to everyone, and in order to take better care of his subjects he tested the honesty of many men. He carefully sought out lovers of justice in various callings, men whom presents would not corrupt. . . . The downfall of oppressors shows how the clergy took up the cases of the poor, and how men who had the authority of knighthood stood up against the powerful and forced everyone to live according to a common law. For the king at various times used abbots, earls, important knights and household officials and companions to hear and examine cases.

[1] From *Select Charters,* ed. W. Stubbs, (Oxford, 1921), p. 156, and from *Pleas of the Crown for the County of Gloucester,* ed. F. W. Maitland (London, 1884), p. XVII.

[Summons of 1221] The king to the sheriff of Worcester, greeting: Summon . . . all archbishops, bishops, abbots, priors, earls and barons, knights and freeholders . . . and from every township four law-abiding men and the reeve [village head] and from every borough twelve law-abiding burgesses . . . and all other men of your district . . . who ought to come before the circuit judges, that they appear before our judges, the abbot of Reading, the abbot of Evesham, Martin of Pateshull, John of Monmouth and their companions on the morrow of the feast of the Holy Trinity at Worcester. . . . And bring before them all pleas of the crown [criminal cases] which have not yet been pleaded . . . and all assizes [cases concerning possession of land] and other pleas which are set down for the coming of the justices. . . .

— Reading No. 48 —

ESTABLISHMENT OF THE DUCHY OF AUSTRIA, 1156[1]

When Frederick Barbarossa (1152-1190) became king of Germany, one of his first problems was to settle a bitter dispute between two of his relatives over the duchy of Bavaria. He solved it by creating a new duchy of Austria out of the eastern part of Bavaria and giving this to an uncle while allowing his nephew to take the rest of Bavaria. Notice the remarkably wide powers possessed by the duke and the small amount of service he owes. The king's power depends on personal relationships with dukes and princes. He is not building a centralized government like those of contemporary English and French kings.

✓ ✓ ✓

In the name of the Holy and Undivided Trinity, Frederick, by divine favor, august emperor of the Romans[2]. . . . The controversy which has long raged between our beloved uncle Henry . . . and our dearest nephew Henry, duke of Saxony, over the duchy of Bavaria is settled in this way. [The first Henry] resigns his claim to Bavaria and we give it immediately as a fief to [Henry] duke of

[1] From *Ausgewählte Urkunden,* ed. by W. Altmann and E. Bernheim (Berlin, 1895), no. 125, p. 277.

[2] The king of Germany was usually elected Holy Roman Emperor. This gave him some rights in Italy, but the real basis of his power was in the German kingdom.

Saxony. The [new] duke of Bavaria hands over to us the March of Austria . . . as margrave Leopold once held it from the duke of Bavaria. And lest in doing this the honor and glory of our beloved uncle might seem to be lessened, by the advice and judgment of the princes . . . we have transformed the March of Austria into a duchy and give it as a fief . . . to our uncle Henry . . . so that he and his wife and their children, male or female, shall hold this duchy of Austria by hereditary right from the kingdom. If, however, our uncle the duke of Austria and his wife should die childless, they may have the right to leave the duchy to whomever they wish.

We also order that no one, great or small, shall presume to exercise any right of justice in the duchy without the consent or permission of the duke. The duke of Austria owes no service for his duchy to the Empire, except that when summoned he shall come to meetings of the [royal] court which the emperor decides to hold in Bavaria. He owes no military service, except in kingdoms or provinces bordering on Austria. . . .

— Reading No. 49 —

LAW OF FREDERICK I ON FEUDALISM IN ITALY, 1158[1]

In Italy, where the power of towns and the importance of commerce increased steadily after the tenth century, feudalism never worked very well. Towns could govern instead of counts; vassals often wanted money instead of land. Fiefs were sold, and military service rapidly lost importance. Lothair III tried to stop this process in 1136; Frederick I repeated and expanded Lothair's law in 1158.

. . . We have heard bitter complaints from the princes of Italy . . . that the fiefs which their vassals hold from them are either used as security for loans or sold without the permission of their lords . . . whereby they lose the service owed, and the honor of the Empire and the strength of our army is diminished.

Having taken the advice of bishops, dukes, margraves, counts . . . and other leading men, we decree, God willing, this permanent law: No one may sell or pledge the whole or part of a fief or alienate it in any way without the consent of his lord from whom he is known to hold the fief. The emperor Lothair already made a law about this, but only forbidding such acts in the future.

We, however, not only forbid such illegal alienation for the future, but revoke and annul all such transactions which have taken place in the past. . . . We also forbid

[1] From *Ausgewählte Urkunden,* ed. by W. Altmann and E. Bernheim (Berlin, 1895), no. 72, pp. 155-156.

those clever tricks, by which fiefs are sold and money is received . . . under color of a pretended sub-enfieff-ment.[2] . . . In such illegal contracts, both seller and buyer shall lose the fief, which then will revert to the lord. The notary who knowingly draws up such a contract shall lose his office . . . and have his hand cut off. . . .

We also ordain, both in Italy and in Germany, that whoever is called for military service by his lord and who fails to come to the army within a reasonable time, or to send an acceptable substitute to his lord, or to pay half of the annual revenue of his fief to his lord,[3] shall lose his fief . . . and the lord of the fief can do as he wishes with it. . . .

[2] Even in countries where the feudal tradition was strong, such as England, land was being sold under pretext of sub-infeudation by the end of the twelfth century.

[3] This is like scutage in England, except that the vassal can pay even if the lord would prefer service.

— Reading No. 50 —

STATUTE IN FAVOR OF THE GERMAN PRINCES, 1232[1]

The emperor Frederick II (1212-1250) tried to base his power on Italy rather than Germany. In order to obtain military support in Italy from the German princes, he granted them many privileges. In this document he, in effect, promises not to try to consolidate royal power in Germany. He gives up rights over towns, commerce, coinage, and justice, rights which were essential to any centralized government. As a result, the German princes became practically independent rulers, just at the time when the Western kings were increasing their control over their great lords.

1) . . . No new castle or town shall be constructed in church lands or by right of advocacy[2] by us or by anyone else under any pretext.

2) New markets shall not be allowed to interfere with old ones. . . .

[1] From *Ausgewählte Urkunden,* ed. W. Altmann and E. Bernheim (Berlin, 1895), no. 10, pp. 21-23.

[2] Churchmen often granted their rights of jurisdiction over laymen to a lord who was called their "advocate." (*See Reading No. 19.*) Such a lord was technically a vassal of the church, but if he were a king or a duke he could act as if the advocacy were part of his own domain. The kings of Germany had been especially successful in acquiring a large number of advocacies.

6) Each prince shall exercise without interference the rights and jurisdiction which he has, according to the custom of his land, in the counties and hundreds which he holds or has granted as fiefs.

7) The local judge shall receive his office from the lord of the land or from the man who has been enfieffed by the lord of the land. . . .

12) We will not receive the serfs of princes and noble men . . . in our towns.

13) Lands and fiefs of princes and nobles . . . which have been occupied by our towns shall be given back. . . .

17) We will not have any new [royal] coins struck in the land of any prince, whereby the coinage of that prince may be injured. . . .

20) No one may receive property as security, which is held as a fief, without the consent of the chief lord [from whom it is held]. . . .

23) Serfs and vassals who wish to go back to their lords, shall not be forced to stay [in our towns] by our officials.

— Reading No. 51 —

SALE OF COUNTY OF MÂCON, FEBRUARY 1239[1]

Mâcon was not a large county, but it occupied a strategic position on one of the main trade-routes to Italy. The count and countess had no children and apparently no great desire to continue to carry the burdens of government themselves. They sold the county to the king for a large lump sum plus a comfortable income. The fact that a county, with its rights of government, could be sold illustrates two things: first, that political power was still considered a private possession, and second, that some feudal lords were becoming more interested in financial profits than in the retention of political power. Notice that the king of France is acquiring rights in his vassals' lands just as the Holy Roman Emperor, king of Germany, is losing them. (See Reading No. 50.)

I, John, count of Mâcon, and I, Alice the countess, his wife, give notice to all men now living and yet to come, that we have sold . . . in perpetuity the county of Mâcon to our dearest lord Louis [IX], the illustrious king of France and his heirs. We have sold the county with everything pertaining to it . . . whether in fiefs or in domains . . . retaining no rights or claims. And the lord king, for

[1] From *Layettes du Trésor des Chartes,* ed. A. Teulet (Paris, 1866), vol. II, no. 2776, p. 400.

this sale . . . gives us 10,000 pounds of Tours[2] in cash and a rent of 1000 pounds a year assigned on lands in Normandy. . . . All this, John the count, and Alice the countess have sworn on holy relics to preserve and observe firmly and inviolably. . . . Done in the year of our Lord 1239 in the month of February.

[2] Pounds of Tours circulated in most of France, outside the old royal domain. They were worth about 1/5 of an English pound. A man with an income of 500 pounds of Tours a year was reasonably well off.

— Reading No. 52 —

AN ALLOD BECOMES A FIEF, 1242[1]

As feudalism developed, more and more landlords became vassals and held their lands as fiefs. This process, however, never involved all the land in any feudal kingdom, except England. Elsewhere, especially in Burgundy, southern France, and Germany, there were many allods, that is, land held with all the rights of private ownership and unburdened by feudal obligation. As feudalism was systematized after 1100, lords tried to persuade owners of allods to surrender their property and receive it back as fiefs. They were reasonably successful in this effort, although allods were never entirely eliminated.

The following example comes from the duchy of Aquitaine, whose duke was also king of England. There are many similar documents which are earlier, but this one has been selected because it shows that an allod could be militarily important. It also shows that the owner of an important allod could gain increased protection at very little cost in service by turning his lands into a fief.

This is the agreement made between the Lord King and Sicard de Montguyon at Bordeaux on Thursday after the Annunciation of the Virgin in the 27th year of the reign of King Henry III (26 March 1242), to wit:

[1] From *Rôles Gascons*, pub. by Francisque Michel (Paris, 1885), vol. I, no. 1211.

The castle of La Clotte, which this Sicard and his ancestors formerly possessed as an allod, shall in the future be held by Sicard and his heirs from the King and his heirs. They shall do homage for it and shall give the service of one lance as relief.[2] If, however, it should happen that Sicard and his knights should lose their lands through war . . . because of the homage and service which are to be done to the King in the future, then the Lord King . . . shall give Sicard reasonable compensation for the lands that are lost. . . . And if perchance a truce is made between the said King and the King of France, a year before the truce ends the said King . . . shall give reasonable aid to Sicard to strengthen his castle and whatever else is necessary to provide against a future war. . . .

[2] Relief, it will be remembered, is the payment made to the lord by the heir of the previous fief-holder. This relief is very low, although a good lance was not inexpensive. (For high reliefs *see Reading No. 30.*)

— Reading No. 53 —

RIGHTS OF JUSTICE OF KNIGHTS AND LESSER LORDS, THIRTEENTH CENTURY[1]

Though the power of kings and great lords increased steadily in the twelfth and thirteenth centuries, they made no attempt to wipe out the rights of justice which rear-vassals had earlier acquired. As long as the superior could hear appeals or intervene directly in important cases, he was quite content to leave the tedious work of settling village quarrels and larcenies to local lords. The two examples given come from Normandy, where the central government had long been very powerful, and Clermont, where the count was a son of the king of France.

✓ ✓ ✓

Knights and freeholders, who have counties or baronies or other feudal dignities, or knight's fees, . . . or any free fiefs, have the right to hold courts for their men in minor cases dealing with chattels and real estate and theft, even if they are of such a nature that they should end in a judicial duel.

✓ ✓ ✓

[1] The first quotation comes from the *Summa de legibus Normannie,* written about 1254-1258, ed. E. J. Tardif (Rouen, 1896), ch. LII, para. 8. The second is from the *Coutumes de Beauvaisis,* written about 1283 by Philippe de Beaumanoir, ed. A. Salmon (Paris, 1879), vol. I, pp. 146-147.

Every man who holds a fief in the county of Clermont has all justice in his fief, high and low, and jurisdiction over his subjects, saving the rights of the count, such as when the subject accuses his lord of failure to do justice. . . .

— Reading No. 54 —

RIGHTS OF JUSTICE OF LESSER LORDS, 1395[1]

A century after Beaumanoir (see Reading No. 51) *it was still assumed that fief-holders normally had rights of justice over their men. This extract comes from a book on French law, written in 1395 by Jean Bouteiller, a member of the highest court in France. This book was still being studied by lawyers in the seventeenth century.*

Natural jurisdiction is the jurisdiction which lords possess by reason of the dignity of lordship over fiefs and noble landholdings. This jurisdiction is hereditary according to the general custom of France. . . . [Some] have high justice, [some] have middle justice, and landholders have low justice and justice over land-rents due to them. For everyone according to the nature of his holding has justice, and can and should settle cases arising in his land as far as his jurisdiction goes. . . . It is fitting that they judge through others than themselves, that is to say, by their feudal subordinates whom they summon and ask to assist them, or through their *bailli* or lieutenant. Appeals can always be made to the sovereign. . . .

[1] From the *Somme rural* by Jean Bouteiller, Title III. In the 1612 edition by Louis Charondas le Caron the quotation is on p. 9.

— Reading No. 55 —

CONSENT TO AIDS IN THIRTEENTH-CENTURY ENGLAND[1]

Besides the aids to which he was entitled in certain closely defined cases (see Reading No. 35), *a feudal lord could ask for financial aid in any emergency. The vassals were free, in theory, to deny or reduce the amount he requested. England was one of the few places where vassals preserved this right and made it more definite during the thirteenth century. Notice that John takes consent for granted in 1207, but that in later documents the need for consent and the way of securing consent are made more and more specific.*

✓ ✓ ✓

The Aid of 1207

The king to all men. . . . Know that by the common counsel and assent of our council at Oxford, it was provided and conceded for the defense of our realm and for the recovery of our rights[2] that every layman in England, no matter whose fief he holds, shall give us in aid a shilling from each mark [=13s.4d.] . . . of annual income or movable property which he holds . . . and the stewards and bailliffs of earls and barons shall swear before our

[1] From *Select Charters,* ed. W. Stubbs (Oxford, 1921), pp. 278, 294-295, 350, 491.

[2] John had just lost most of his French fiefs to king Philip Augustus, and was trying to recover them.

justices as to the value of the income and chattels of their lords. . . .

Magna Carta, 1215

Ch. 12 No scutage or aid shall be imposed on our kingdom except by the common counsel of the realm, except to ransom our body, make our eldest son a knight, and marry our eldest daughter. . . .

Ch. 14 And to secure the common counsel of the realm for imposing an aid, except in the three aforesaid cases . . . we will summon archbishops, bishops, abbots, earls and greater barons by our sealed letters, and we will also summon by our sheriffs . . . all those who hold directly from us . . . and in all the letters the reason for the summons shall be expressly stated . . . and the business shall proceed on the day assigned by the summons according to the advice of those present, even if all those summoned do not come.

Grant of Aid in 1225

In return for this concession and the grant of these liberties [a confirmation of Magna Carta by Henry III] . . . the archbishops, bishops, abbots, priors, earls, barons, knights, free tenants, and all of our kingdom have given us one fifteenth of all their chattels.

Confirmation of the Charters, 1297

And we [Edward I] have also granted for us and our heirs to archbishops, bishops, abbots, priors . . . and to earls, and barons and to the whole community of the land, that we will take no aids . . . from our kingdom except by the common consent of all the kingdom and for the common welfare of the realm. . . .

— Reading No. 56 —

EXPENSES OF THE FRANCO-ARAGONESE WAR OF 1285[1]

In 1285 Philip III, King of France, attempted to conquer Aragon for his son, Charles of Valois. This attack was made under pressure from the Pope, who wished to punish the King of Aragon for his conquest of Sicily, a papal fief. Those who went on the expedition had all the incentives and privileges of Crusaders. Yet, as the following documents show, King Philip had to pay very large sums to secure military service from the feudal group, even those of highest rank. At the same time, it is evident that he was eager to have as many lords and knights as possible in his army.

The first document is a summary of total expenses; the second is an extract from a long list of individual payments for support of the army.

✓ ✓ ✓

Summary of Expenses for the Aragon Expedition

First, by account of Master Pierre de Condé, wages for knights of the king's household—170,341 pounds of Tours.[2]

[1] *Recueil des historiens des Gaules et de la France,* ed. N. de Wailly and L. Delisle (Paris, 1855, 1865), vol. xxi, p. 516, vol. xxii, pp. 480-481.

[2] There were two kinds of royal money in France in the thirteenth century, the pound of Paris for the old royal domain, and the pound of Tours for newly acquired provinces. Four pounds of Paris equalled five pounds of Tours.

For the wages of knights not of the household—109,254 pounds of Tours.

For the wages of knights of France—10,618 pounds of Tours.

For the wages of knights of Toulouse—17,961 pounds of Tours.

For the wages of [ordinary] horsemen and footmen—243,720 pounds of Tours.

Each horseman had five shillings a day and each footman one shilling of Paris.

Individual Payments for Support of the Army

The lord Dreux of Plessey, according to agreement, 20 pounds of Tours.

The viscount of Melun, according to agreement, 50 pounds of Tours.

The lord of Choiseul . . . 200 pounds of Tours.

The lord of Cressonsacq, according to agreement, 40 pounds of Tours.

Lord Guillaume Painel, according to agreement, 20 pounds of Tours.

Lord Pons de Bonac . . . 60 pounds of Tours.

Lord Jean of Walencourt . . . 30 pounds of Tours.

The vidame of Chartres . . . 30 pounds of Tours.

The count of Burgundy . . . 100 pounds of Tours.[3]

The duke of Brabant . . . 300 pounds of Tours.[3]

The bishop of Langres . . . 50 pounds of Tours.

[3] Both the duke of Brabant and the count of Burgundy were princes of the Holy Roman Empire. Kings were not restricted to their own subjects when it came to hiring soldiers, and the western part of the Empire was for centuries an especially good recruiting area.

— Reading No. 57 —

A MILITARY INDENTURE, 30 MAY 1416[1]

This was the usual form of contract used in raising armed forces in England in the fourteenth and fifteenth centuries. Notice that the king hires only the three knights; they must raise the rest of the company. The great lords of the kingdom also raised armed bands in this way. Service was given for money and the hope of booty, but the officers of the companies were usually, as in this case, of good family.

✓ ✓ ✓

This indenture, made between our sovereign lord the King, on the one hand, and Nicholas Montgomery, Richard Hastings, and John Osbaldeston, knights, on the other, witnesseth:

The said knights are retained by our lord the King to accompany him on expedition overseas which he will undertake in his own person, and there to serve him in war with nine men-at-arms (themselves included) and 18 archers well and suitably armed . . . for a quarter of a year beginning Monday the 22nd day of June. And each of the said knights shall have two shillings a day and each of the other men-at-arms one shilling a day, and each of the said archers half-a-shilling a day for their wages. . . . And concerning booty and capture of great lords

[1] From *Lord Hastings' Indentured Retainers* by W. H. Dunham, Jr. (New Haven, 1955), p. 136.

[for ransom] . . . the king shall have the part which belongs to him according to the custom of ancient times. . . .

— Reading No. 58 —

THE PROVISIONS OF OXFORD, 1258[1]

By 1258 the barons of England had lost confidence in the policies of Henry III. They wanted to exert a continuing influence on policy and to reform the administration. To do this, they tried to transform their old duty *of advising the king at his request into a* right *of consent to all important decisions. The text of the agreement they imposed on the king is badly garbled, but it is clear that they wanted an elected council of barons to have full power to check and control the king.*

✓ ✓ ✓

It is to be remembered that . . . there shall be three parliaments[2] a year. . . . The elected councillors of the king shall come to these three parliaments, even if they are not summoned, to consider the state of the realm and to treat of the common needs of the kingdom and of the king. . . .

It is also to be remembered that the community of barons shall choose twelve noteworthy men who will come to parliaments . . . when the king or his council shall summon them to consider the needs of the king and the kingdom. And the community shall accept as final any

[1] From *Select Charters,* ed. W. Stubbs (Oxford, 1921), p. 383.

[2] Parliament at this time was simply a very full meeting of the king's court, which dealt primarily with difficult legal problems.

decision made by the twelve. This is to save the community the expense [of coming to meetings].

Fifteen men shall be named [by a committee established by agreement between the king and the barons] and these fifteen shall form the king's Council. . . . They shall have power to advise the king in good faith concerning the government of the realm and all things concerning the king and the kingdom. They shall also have power to reform and correct all things which they think need reform or correction. And they have power over the Chief Justice and all other officials. And if they cannot all be present, that which is done by the majority shall be final and binding.

RECOMMENDED READING

In English:

Marc Bloch, *Feudal Society,* London and Chicago, 1961.

Rushton Coulborn, ed., *Feudalism in History,* Princeton, 1956.

D. C. Douglas, *Feudal Documents from the Abbey of Bury St. Edmunds,* London, 1932.

D. C. Douglas, "The Norman Conquest and English Feudalism," *Economic History Review* IX (1939), pp. 128 ff.

D. C. Douglas, *William the Conqueror,* Berkeley, 1964.

F. L. Ganshof, *Feudalism,* London, 1952.

C. W. Hollister, *Anglo-Saxon Military Institutions,* New York, 1962.

Bryce Lyon, *From Fief to Indenture,* Cambridge, 1957.

K. B. McFarlane, "Bastard Feudalism," *Bull. Inst. for Hist. Research* XX (1945).

Charles Odegaard, *Vassi and Fideles in the Carolingian Empire,* Cambridge, 1945.

Ch. Petit-Dutaillis, *The Feudal Monarchy in France and England,* London, 1936.

J. O. Prestwich, "War and Finance in the Anglo-Norman State," *Transactions of the Royal Historical Society,* series 5, IV (1954), pp. 453 ff.

H. G. Richardson and G. O. Sayles, *The Governance of Mediaeval England,* Edinburgh, 1963.

J. H. Round, *Feudal England,* London, 1909.

F. M. Stenton, *The First Century of English Feudalism,* Oxford, 1932.

Carl Stephenson, *Medieval Feudalism,* Ithaca, 1942.

Carl Stephenson, *Medieval Institutions,* Ithaca, 1954.

J. R. Strayer, "The Development of Feudal Institutions," in *Twelfth Century Europe,* ed. M. Clagett, G. Post, and R. R. Reynolds, pp. 77 ff., Madison, 1961.

J. R. Strayer, "Two Levels of Feudalism," in *Life and Thought in the Early Middle Ages,* ed. R. S. Hoyt, Minneapolis, 1965.

In Foreign Languages:

R. Boutruche, *Seigneurie et féodalité,* Paris, 1959.

J. Calmette, *La société féodale,* Paris, 1947.

J. Dhondt, *Etudes sur la naissance des principautés territoriales en France,* Bruges, 1948.

G. Duby, "La noblesse dans la France médiévale," *Révue historique* 226 (1961), pp. 15 ff.

G. Duby, *La société au XIe et XIIe siècles dans la région mâconnaise,* Paris, 1953.

F. L. Ganshof, "L'origine des rapports féodo-vassaliques," *I Problemi della civilta carolingia,* Spoleto, 1954, pp. 46 ff.

F. L. Ganshof, "Les relations féodo-vassaliques aux temps post-carolingiens," *I Problemi communi dell'Europa post-carolingia,* Spoleto, 1955, pp. 67 ff.

A. Guilhiermoz, *Essai sur les origines de la noblesse en France,* Paris, 1902.

W. Kienast, *Untertaneneid und Treuvorbehalt,* Weimar, 1952.

J. F. Lemarignier, "La dislocation du Pagus," *Mélanges Halphen,* Paris, 1951.

J. F. Lemarignier, "Les fidèles du roi de France," *Recueil Clovis Brunel,* Paris, 1955.

J. F. Lemarignier, "Structures monastiques et structures politiques de la France de la fin du Xe et des debuts du XIe siècles," *Il Monachismo nell Alto Medioevo,* Spoleto, 1957, pp. 365 ff.

H. Mitteis, *Lehnrecht und Staatsgewalt,* Weimar, 1933.

H. Mitteis, *Der Staat des hohen Mittelalters,* Weimar, 1955.

J. Richard, *Les ducs de Bourgogne et la formation du duché,* Paris, 1954.

K. F. Werner, "Untersuchungen zur Frühzeit des Französischen Fürstentums," *Die Welt als Geschichte,* XVIII (1958), pp. 256 ff., XIX (1959), pp. 146 ff., XX (1960), pp. 87 ff.

INDEX

VAN NOSTRAND REINHOLD ANVIL BOOKS

1 *MAKING OF MODERN FRENCH MIND*—Kohn
2 *THE AMERICAN REVOLUTION*—Morris
3 *THE LATE VICTORIANS*—Ausubel
4 *WORLD IN THE 20th CENTURY*—Rev. Ed.—Snyder
5 *50 DOCUMENTS OF THE 20th CENTURY*—Snyder
6 *THE AGE OF REASON*—Snyder
7 *MARX AND THE MARXISTS*—Hook
8 *NATIONALISM*—Kohn
9 *MODERN JAPAN*—Rev. Ed.—Tiedemann
10 *50 DOCUMENTS OF THE 19th CENTURY*—Snyder
11 *CONSERVATISM*—Viereck
12 *THE PAPACY*—Corbett
13 *AGE OF THE REFORMATION*—Bainton
14 *DOCUMENTS IN AMERICAN HISTORY*—Rev. Ed.--Morris
15 *CONTEMPORARY AFRICA*—Rev. Ed.—Wallbank
16 *THE RUSSIAN REVOLUTIONS OF 1917*—Curtiss
17 *THE GREEK MIND*—Agard
18 *BRITISH CONSTITUTIONAL HISTORY SINCE 1832*—Schuyler and Weston
19 *THE NEGRO IN THE U.S., Vol. I: A History to 1945*—Logan
20 *AMERICAN CAPITALISM*—Hacker
21 *LIBERALISM*—Schapiro
22 *THE FRENCH REVOLUTION, 1789-1799*—Gershoy
23 *HISTORY OF MODERN GERMANY*—Snyder
24 *HISTORY OF MODERN RUSSIA*—Kohn
25 *NORTH ATLANTIC CIVILIZATION*—Kraus
26 *NATO*—Salvadori
27 *DOCUMENTS IN U.S. FOREIGN POLICY*—Brockway
28 *AMERICAN FARMERS' MOVEMENTS*—Shannon
29 *HISTORIC DECISIONS OF SUPREME COURT*—Swisher
30 *MEDIEVAL TOWN*—Mundy and Riesenberg
31 *REVOLUTION AND REACTION 1848-1852*—Bruun
32 *CONTEMPORARY SOUTHEAST ASIA*—Buss
33 *HISTORIC DOCUMENTS OF W. W. I*—Snyder
34 *HISTORIC DOCUMENTS OF W. W. II*—Langsam
35 *ROMAN MIND AT WORK*—MacKendrick
36 *SHORT HISTORY OF CANADA*—Masters
37 *WESTWARD MOVEMENT IN U.S.*—Billington
38 *DOCUMENTS IN MEDIEVAL HISTORY*—Downs
39 *BASIC HISTORY OF AMERICAN BUSINESS*—Rev. Ed.—Cochran
40 *DOCUMENTS IN CANADIAN HISTORY*—Talman
41 *FOUNDATIONS OF ISRAEL*—Janowsky
42 *MODERN CHINA*—Rowe
43 *BASIC HISTORY OF OLD SOUTH*—Stephenson
44 *THE BENELUX COUNTRIES*—Eyck
45 *MEXICO AND THE CARIBBEAN*—Rev. Ed.—Hanke
46 *SOUTH AMERICA*—Rev. Ed.—Hanke
47 *SOVIET FOREIGN POLICY, 1917-1941*—Kennan
48 *THE ERA OF REFORM, 1830-1860*—Commager
49 *EARLY CHRISTIANITY*—Bainton
50 *RISE AND FALL OF THE ROMANOVS*—Mazour
51 *CARDINAL DOCUMENTS IN BRITISH HISTORY*—Schuyler and Weston
52 *HABSBURG EMPIRE 1804-1918*—Kohn
53 *CAVOUR AND UNIFICATION OF ITALY*—Salvadori
54 *ERA OF CHARLEMAGNE*—Easton and Wieruszowski
55 *MAJOR DOCUMENTS IN AMERICAN ECONOMIC HISTORY, Vol. I*—Hacker
56 *MAJOR DOCUMENTS IN AMERICAN ECONOMIC HISTORY, Vol. II*—Hacker
57 *HISTORY OF THE CONFEDERACY*—Vandiver
58 *COLD WAR DIPLOMACY*—Graebner
59 *MOVEMENTS OF SOCIAL DISSENT IN MODERN EUROPE—Schapiro*
60 *MEDIEVAL COMMERCE*—Adelson
61 *THE PEOPLE'S REPUBLIC OF CHINA*—Buss
62 *WORLD COMMUNISM*—Hook
63 *ISLAM AND THE WEST*—Hitti